SEMINAR STUDIES IN HISTORY

Editor: Patrick Richardson

The LEVELLERS

SEMINAR STUDIES IN HISTORY

Editor: Patrick Richardson

A full list of titles in this
series will be found on the
back cover of this book

SEMINAR STUDIES IN HISTORY

The LEVELLERS

Howard Shaw

LONGMANS

LONGMANS, GREEN AND CO LTD
48 Grosvenor Street, London, W1
ASSOCIATED COMPANIES, BRANCHES AND REPRESENTATIVES
THROUGHOUT THE WORLD

© Longmans, Green and Co., Ltd 1968

First published 1968

PRINTED IN GREAT BRITAIN BY NEILL & CO LTD, EDINBURGH

Contents

Acknowledgements

I should like to thank the Master and Fellows of Emmanuel College, Cambridge, who elected me to a Schoolmaster Fellow-Commonership to write this book; also the Head Master and Governors of Harrow School, who generously allowed me a sabbatical term to take advantage of this election.

HOWARD SHAW

We are indebted to the following for permission to reproduce copyright material:

The British Museum Trustees for extracts from seven of the *Leveller Manifestoes* of the Puritan Revolution (Thomason Collection), which are reprinted in *Leveller Manifestoes of the Puritan Revolution* by Dr. D. Wolfe, published by Humanities Press Inc. (Reprint edition 1967); Royal Historical Society for two documents from *The Clarke Papers* edited by Sir. C. H. Firth (The Camden Society 1891-1901).

Introduction to the Series

The seminar method of teaching is being used increasingly in VI forms and at universities. It is a way of learning in smaller groups through discussion, designed both to get away from and to supplement the basic lecture techniques. To be successful, the members of a seminar must be informed—or else, in the unkind phrase of a cynic—it can be a 'pooling of ignorance'. The chapter in the textbook of English or European history by its nature cannot provide material in this depth, but at the same time the full academic work may be too long and perhaps too advanced for students at this level.

For this reason we have invited practising teachers in universities, schools and colleges of further education to contribute short studies on specialised aspects of British and European history with these special needs and pupils of this age in mind. For this series the authors have been asked to provide, in addition to their basic analysis, a full selection of documentary material of all kinds and an up-to-date and comprehensive bibliography. Both these sections are referred to in the text, but it is hoped that they will prove to be valuable teaching and learning aids in themselves.

Note on the System of References:

A bold number in round brackets (**5**) in the text refers the reader to the corresponding entry in the Bibliography section at the end of the book.

A bold number in square brackets, preceded by 'doc' [**docs 6, 8**] refers the reader to the corresponding items in the section of Documents, which follows the main text.

PATRICK RICHARDSON
General Editor

Part One

THE
BACKGROUND

1 Puritanism

It is a truism that each generation sees the past in the light of its own experiences and it is not surprising that the present materialist age has sought to impose on the English Revolution interpretations which leave little room for motives of the spirit. In recent years the Civil War period has been the subject of intensive economic and sociological analysis and, as a result, Puritanism, once seen as the prime cause of the upheaval, has tended to become merely a moral cloak for men whose interests were essentially mundane (e.g. **34**). However, it is a mistake to carry this too far. There were, of course, many reasons why men adopted Puritan beliefs, but to interpret the fiery idealism of seventeenth-century Puritanism solely in terms of the social ambitions or grievances of particular classes is to miss the peculiar qualities of Puritanism itself. Certainly any study of the Levellers must begin with a survey of their spiritual rather than their secular origins, for although they frequently seemed more concerned with the fate of man in this world rather than the next there can be no doubt that Puritanism was the main source of their energy and ideas.

Calvinism represented the mainstream of Puritanism and it contained a fundamental ambiguity: on the one hand, the doctrine of predestination led to the assumption that the elect—those 'saints' predestined to salvation—should rule as an authoritarian theocracy; on the other hand, the belief in the equality of the elect before God fostered an egalitarian spirit which could lead to the questioning of a social as well as a religious hierarchy. Both these tendencies can be seen in the English Revolution.

The idea that the elect should rule emerged in two forms, one conservative, the other, paradoxically, revolutionary. The Presbyterians, English heirs of the Calvinist tradition and leaders of the reactionary wing of the alliance that had defeated the king, hoped to establish a rigidly intolerant Church which would slip smoothly into the social and economic structure of the country as it stood.

3

Later, the millenarian Fifth Monarchists, who interpreted the overthrow of Charles and the ensuing turmoil as the overture to Christ's reign on earth, saw it as their duty to prepare for His coming by attacking the evils of the society they saw around them. As a minority group seeking popular support they paid lip-service to talk of liberty and freedom of conscience, but, in fact, taking their text from *Revelation* 20, 'The Saints shall reign with him a thousand years', regarded themselves as a revolutionary *élite* heading for authoritarian rule.

So the Presbyterians and Fifth Monarchists moved towards the rule of the saints, but from the beginning Calvinism contained ideas of equality that were bound to undermine the claims of this spiritual aristocracy. The elect were equal, but who were the elect? Calvinist preachers obviously found it desirable to hold out the hope that members of their congregations might be saints and it was not too difficult for aspiring converts to convince themselves they were destined for the delights of paradise rather than the horrors of eternal damnation. As a result the circle of the godly few widened, carrying with it the dangerous idea that all the fortunates gathered within, whatever their status in society, were equal before the throne of God.

Closely linked with this equality was the Puritan attitude to the Scriptures. Throughout the Reformation the main weapon used to attack the Catholic Church was the Bible. Rome had strayed from the Word; the reformers would return to it, destroying anything for which there was not a strict scriptural basis. For years, the argument ran, the papal hierarchy had conspired to hide the truth by making the Bible a mystery soluble only through the ministrations of a priest; now, following the teaching of Luther and Calvin and with translations in the vernacular available, men could see for themselves the path to salvation. Thus there developed a new personal relationship between the ordinary man and his God, a change which drastically increased the importance of the individual conscience. If it was capable of understanding the Word of God, why should it not cast a critical eye on other matters previously considered beyond its competence? Here, in the equality of the elect and the elevation of the individual, lay the origins of Leveller thought.

Furthermore, the saint was expected to act; he did not sit at home in quiet contemplation of his good fortune. He had been called, but this great privilege carried duties as well as rights. As a member of the *élite* it was his task to do everything in his power to advance God's kingdom. Puritan use of the imagery of warfare in sermons and pamphlets illustrates this sense of struggle. The true saint was a soldier, disciplined and vigilant, on guard against the wiles of Satan, fearlessly attacking sin in all its forms. 'The condition of the child of God', wrote Thomas Taylor, 'is military in this life' (**28**). This attitude led the Puritan to question all the traditional forms he saw around him; he became a man of action, of reform, of experiment. Predestination left no room for good works as a *means* of salvation, but they soon became a distinguishing characteristic of those who considered themselves saved already. The Puritan found himself armed with an ideology that encouraged him to challenge his social, economic and political superiors.

These beliefs inevitably affected the personality of the individual. As one of the chosen the Puritan claimed a special relationship with the Almighty and this gave him enormous confidence: 'If God be for us, who can be against us?' Such assurance bred, at best, courage, self-discipline and a sense of purpose; at worst, a narrow self-righteous bigotry. Ironically, John Lilburne, the Leveller leader, and Oliver Cromwell, his most determined opponent, may both be cited as outstanding examples of the way in which Puritanism could toughen the individual character.

These influences sprang from Geneva and the main body of Reformation thought, but no genealogy of the Leveller party would be complete without mention of the Anabaptist tradition. Although the name Anabaptist was used loosely to cover a variety of religious opinions that appeared in central Europe in the 1520s, certain common beliefs that are relevant here may be identified. The Anabaptists shared with Calvinism the doctrine of election, but, unlike the latter, wanted the complete separation of church and state. For them the church was a pure body of believers withdrawn into a voluntary congregation—a withdrawal almost monastic in its exclusion of the world. The church was a 'holy community' setting the highest standards of Christian behaviour, while the state, by its very nature inclusive of everybody, was inevitably contaminated with sin. This led them, logically, to be the first church to make religious toleration a basic tenet of their creed. Clearly a tainted authority could not dictate to the men of God. The Anabaptists rejected infant baptism on the grounds that each

5

individual should take the responsibility for joining the church when he reached the age of discretion; they believed in equality, both of men and women; they were originally pacifists and condemned capital punishment; occasionally they held goods in common and lived without money or wages. In their day and age these ideals were heresy of a high order and they aroused hostility from the start, particularly as they tended to be held by the lower classes. Unfortunately for the Anabaptists, most of whom remained loyal to their pacifist beliefs, extremists confirmed the authorities in their suspicions. Thomas Münzer—not an Anabaptist but very near to them—played a prominent part in the German Peasant War of 1525; at Münster in 1534 Jan of Leyden seized the city hall and tried to establish the New Jerusalem by force of arms; elsewhere wild prophets foretold the end of the world. Persecution was vigorous and cruel; adherents of the faith were hunted down and executed wherever they could be found. The name 'Anabaptist' became a term of execration throughout Europe. It is not, therefore, surprising that there was bitter opposition to the Levellers when they tried to translate several key aspects of the Anabaptist tradition into a political programme (**13**).

In the generations before the Civil War, Puritanism in England developed in several directions. We have already noted the conflict within Calvinist doctrine between authoritarianism and ideas which may be described loosely as democratic. This contradiction, masked in Geneva where rigid uniformity was imposed from on high, was clearly revealed in the years following Elizabeth's religious settlement. In 1559 many Marian exiles hoped to establish a fully 'reformed' Church; they were disappointed. Elizabeth, concerned more with national unity than religious uniformity, created a hybrid firmly under her own control. Nevertheless, it was on the whole a tolerant Church and the Puritans—whether moderates, who accepted the episcopacy but opposed vestments, or Presbyterians, who wanted a full Calvinist system from top to bottom—were allowed a good deal of freedom to spread their beliefs within its fabric. Here was the Puritan preacher's dilemma: he could teach, but he had no influence over the disciplinary machinery his doctrines required; he could not, therefore, restrain the forces he set free (**18**).

He taught that anyone might be a saint, and that all could discover God by reading the Bible. The theory was that if men studied the Bible in a spirit of honest inquiry they were bound to be unanimous over the truths revealed there. In fact something very different happened. The Bible was found to be open to as many interpretations as there were minds to study it. Instead of building a powerful community united in doctrine and ready to erect the New Jerusalem at a moment's notice, the Puritans found themselves unwittingly fostering the idea that anyone could get to heaven in his own way. It only required a persuasive teacher to become convinced of some special insight into God's intentions and he could collect a band of followers to form a 'church' of his own. Hence the Puritans found themselves fighting on two fronts: against the Anglican Church, which had no intention of succumbing to a full Calvinist takeover; and against the small sects that tended to spiral away from the left of their own movement. This centrifugal tendency towards separatism was apparent from the first, but its full consequences did not take effect until the Anglican Church was overthrown in the 1640s. Then Puritanism, previously held together by its opposition to the Elizabethan settlement, disintegrated into warring factions of rival saints.

It is in these radical sects that one must seek the immediate origins of the Leveller movement for here the egalitarian ideas implicit in Calvinism developed freely. Orthodox Calvinism emphasised the individual spiritual experience but crushed the liberty of the individual will with the weight of predestination. The separatists tended to be more optimistic and more logical. If all men were free to find God in their own hearts with the aid of Scripture, each man must have some control over his eternal destiny; he must, in fact, be free to accept or reject the grace offered by God. This voluntarism not only raised the status of the conscience yet further; it also condemned by implication any attempt by the civil magistrate to interfere with the individual while seeking his God—a condemnation which could readily be supported by using the New Testament against the Old. Here was the basis of the demand for religious toleration which first brought the Leveller leaders together in 1645 [**doc. 1**].

Furthermore, the sects were often democratic in organisation, even to the extent of giving women an equal share in governing the congregation; frequently they were bound together by a written contract to which all members agreed. Relying on direct inspiration by the Holy Spirit, the sects encouraged lay preaching and at all times deprecated the authority of a ministerial caste. Their opponents, Anglicans and Presbyterians alike, reviled them all as Anabaptists. Some were, and an English strain of Anabaptism developed rapidly during the Civil War. The Leveller leader Richard Overton was originally an Anabaptist.

Historians disagree over the definition of Puritanism. It will be apparent that it is used here in its widest sense, covering all those who considered that the Anglican Church had not swung far enough from Rome. This included a broad spectrum of belief, from the Presbyterians on the right to the separatists on the left. The common factor was opposition to things as they stood; in this sense Puritanism was a state of mind rather than a specific doctrine. Thanks to the entanglement of religion and politics, opposition in one field meant opposition in the other also; crown and bishops leaned on each other for support—eventually they were overthrown together. Hence the Puritans helped to form a climate of opinion critical of all aspects of the Tudor and Stuart establishment; they were, as Mr Walzer has said, 'oppositional men' (**28**). Perhaps John Lilburne was the most 'oppositional' man of all.

In the first half of the seventeenth century religion continued to dominate men's thinking just as it had done before the Reformation; it was an all-embracing force that shaped their ideas and gave meaning to their lives. For this reason it is right to deal with Puritanism first, but it is unreal to look at it in isolation as we have done so far. Puritanism provided an ideological discipline that transcended older loyalties and stimulated criticism of accepted standards and institutions; it gave men confidence, courage and a feverish enthusiasm; it stirred up notions of equality. But revolutionary movements need more than abstract ideas and zeal. The Levellers might not have emerged at all, and would certainly never have exerted the influence they did, had political, social and economic circumstances not been favourable. Puritanism gave the Levellers their initial impetus; secular conditions enabled them to flourish (**18, 19, 28**).

2 Social and Economic Background

Judged by modern standards, seventeenth-century society was rigid and static. It was widely accepted that its hierarchical structure was part of a divine plan and reflected the harmony of a universe in which each creature had its place. King, nobles, gentry, yeomen and peasants, all had their degree and were not expected to stray from it; they were an integral part of the Great Chain of Being, the theory that God in his wisdom had long ago fitted all things into a natural order which did not change. Within this hierarchy the most fundamental division was between those who were 'gentlemen' and those who were not, the distinction being largely a matter of whether one did, or did not, have to soil one's hands with manual labour. Gentlemen, from peers of the realm to small landowners, were the natural rulers of the countryside. They owned the bulk of the land, they filled practically all administrative offices, and they sent their representatives to Parliament to see that national affairs were conducted along the right lines; as lords of the manor they were the focal point of local power in an age which still thought largely in parochial terms. Symbols of the social superiority of gentlemen were many: they were entitled to a coat-of-arms and carried weapons; they expected preferential treatment before the law; certain sports and forms of dress were reserved for them; until Laud stopped it, gentry frequently drank vintage wine at communion while their servants had *vin ordinaire* (**13**).

Of course it was possible to rise or fall in the hierarchy, and even to cross the great divide between 'gentle' and 'simple'. A fortunate career at Court, a carefully arranged marriage, occasionally sheer hard work or ability, could lead to an improvement of status. Lionel Cranfield began as an apprentice and ended as an earl, and there are plenty of other examples; indeed, it has recently been shown that the period 1560–1640 was one of comparatively high social mobility (**42**). Nevertheless, it was essentially a graded society and none hastened to preserve his privileges as anxiously as he who had

9

only recently attained them; great differences of wealth and degree were looked upon as normal. The common man looked about him, saw that men were unequal, and, on the whole, accepted the rank to which it had pleased God to call him.

Phlegmatic acceptance of a particular rank in society did not necessarily imply acceptance of the hardships that might go with it; far from it. The history of the Middle Ages is punctuated with the blind revolts of men who found their lot too hard to bear. A bad harvest, a new tax, excessive demands by a feudal lord: all these might spur an illiterate peasantry to wreak vengeance on those they considered responsible for their wrongs. Just occasionally, as in 1381, a revolt became more dangerous for the upper classes when immediate economic grievances became linked with wider social aims. 'When Adam delved and Eve span, who was then the gentleman?' But this was the exception. In general, these spasms of disaffection were the pangs of a primitive economy faced with the natural hazards of weather, plague or war; they had no long-term programme. Puritanism, as we have seen, was to provide the ordinary man with an ideology that could form the basis of a revolutionary political platform.

In the hundred years before the Civil War, two disruptive forces were at work which affected all classes of the hierarchical ladder: the massive inflation and the growth in population. From 1500 to 1640 prices rose between 400 and 650 per cent, with food prices well in the lead; wages lagged behind. This had far reaching consequences, both for agriculture and industry. Anyone who had anything to sell could keep himself on the crest of the mounting price wave; those who depended on fixed incomes tended to be submerged as their money dwindled in value. The sharp rise in population was also important. Exact figures are not available but Professor Lawrence Stone suggests that between 1500 and 1620 the population of England and Wales nearly doubled, to reach a total of about five million (**42**). This increase inevitably stimulated the price rise and at the same time helped to depress wages by adding to the labour force.

The great mass of the population at this time got its living from the land. At the top were the landowners, large and small, who lived on rents; in the middle, less clearly defined, were the independent farmers, some qualifying as gentry, others as yeomen; beneath these came the leaseholders, the copyholders, and the tenants-at-will;

below them again, forming the broad base of the pyramid, were the wage labourers. Of the groups in this oversimplified picture, the small freehold farmers in the middle of the scale were probably in the best position, though their numbers were almost certainly not as great as was once thought. As owners of their land, they had security of tenure and were able to take full advantage of the rising market, particularly those who had capital behind them for improvements. It was the landowner living on rents, the copyholder whose rights were in doubt, and the labourer living on wages who felt the inflationary draught. Of these, it is the copyholder who concerns us here.

In the fifteenth century, when prices were stable and labour was relatively expensive, it had paid landowners to lease out their land; but in the sixteenth and early seventeenth centuries they could no longer afford such a relaxed attitude. If a landowner was to survive, he had to exploit his land to the utmost and ensure that he, and not the tenant with a fixed rent, enjoyed the profits of production. This could be done in two main ways: first, by farming his estates efficiently himself; second, by letting out land on short leases that could be renewed regularly to keep step with the inflation. The copyholder stood in the way of both these processes.

The copyholder was a descendant of the former villein and he held strips in open fields from the lord of the manor. His holding depended on his possession of a copy of the relevant entry in the manor roll and was subject to the customs of that particular manor. Though it would be unwise to generalise about the fortunes of the copyholders, for their situation varied from place to place and there are many examples of those who profited from the inflationary market, it is clear that some were doing badly. If the copyholder had no documentary evidence of his rights, an unscrupulous landlord would not have much difficulty in removing him. If his copy was good, the landowner would have to wait until the owner died and his heir took over; then, unless the terms of the original copyhold dictated fixed payments, he could raise the rent, which had often remained unchanged for generations, and exact a large entry fine. Previously the custom of the manor had dictated moderate payments in both cases, but such feudal notions were fading and the copyholder might find himself with a rent or fine far beyond his means. Nor was there always an obligation for the lord to renew the tenancy, and when the copy expired it was sometimes possible for him to take back the land. Some copyholders, particularly those with large holdings or who held freehold land as well, resisted strenuously and successfully, occasionally turning copyhold land into freehold tenure with a cash payment; others, usually the poorer men who had no savings to draw upon, were forced off the land and sank to the level of the landless labourer (**33**).

So the smaller copyholder was frequently ejected from land his family had farmed for centuries. His resentment was increased, and his economic position further endangered, by the enclosure that often took place on the land that he, and others like him, had left. In their drive for efficiency, landowners, prosperous yeomen as well as lords of the manor, had for many years been enclosing strips into fields, sometimes for sheep, sometimes for arable to feed the growing population. The poorer peasants, often not far above subsistence level and below it in a bad year, lost on all counts: enclosure for any purpose meant a purge of strip-holders, and enclosure for sheep meant less employment and depopulation. Moreover, the lord of the manor frequently nibbled at the common land of the village and in some ways this hit the cottager hardest of all, for here, from time immemorial, he had gathered fuel for the winter and put out a few beasts to graze. Hostility to enclosures had long been widespread and successive governments, acutely aware of the dangers of social unrest, had made frequent, and ineffectual, efforts to limit landowners' enclosing activities. The extent of enclosure varied from place to place and should not be exaggerated, but it was clearly a constant irritant. There were enclosure riots in the Midlands in 1607, and in the early years of the Civil War bands of peasants pulled down hedges all over the country.

Here in the countryside, with wages constantly dropping behind prices (it is estimated that the purchasing power of wages had dropped by something like two thirds in the sixteenth century) there was a permanent pool of discontent. The Levellers' failure to exploit it fully must stand as one of the main reasons why they were defeated so easily. They were certainly not ignorant of the grievances. Destruction of recent enclosures was demanded in several of their pamphlets, including *The Case of the Army Truly Stated*. The plight of the copyholders was recognised in a scheme put forward in 1648, just before the second Civil War, when the Levellers proposed abolition of all copyholds, the holders to be given the chance to buy the freehold. Nevertheless, the Levellers never mobilised rural opinion as they might have done; in spite of close contact with supporters in Buckinghamshire and Hertfordshire, they were essentially an urban movement and even when constructing a political platform seemed strangely blind to agrarian complaints. This was a great weakness. Not only were copyholders numerous and ripe for agitation; they were also going to be given the vote under the Levellers' franchise plans—a vote they would never use with any independence while saddled with a 'base tenure' that effectively tied them to their landlord (**13**).

The pressure that forced some copyholders downwards had its parallel in the industrial sphere. The inflationary century before 1640 had seen significant industrial expansion. Coal, tin, lead, copper and iron production had risen; shipbuilding, brick-making, soap-boiling, salt-refining and dyeing—all increased output to meet the needs of the growing population and to take advantage of the seller's market. But such expansion needed capital and this came in the main from large merchants and landowners; the smaller man found he could not compete. By the seventeenth century the woollen industry, the oldest and most important of English industries, had for some time been completely dominated by the capitalist clothier. Other industries followed suit. For the capitalist, his position of economic superiority meant political and social power as well. George Lilburne, John Lilburne's uncle, is a good example. As chandler, grocer, mercer, owner of collieries and land, he held a commanding position in Sunderland—a position strong enough to take as many members of the borough to the side of parliament in the war as a substantial royalist gentleman took to the king (**48**). This decline of the small operator was taking place all over the country; it was mirrored and magnified in London.

It is impossible to understand the Civil War or the Leveller movement if one does not grasp the importance of London. Its recent growth in population had been remarkable. Many towns had increased in size but London outstripped them all. From a figure of about 60,000 early in the sixteenth century, it had risen to something in the region of 350,000 by 1650. Swollen by the surplus population of the countryside, it sprawled five miles along the northern bank of the Thames and three along the south. A wide belt of country was dedicated to providing its food—its corn consumption more than doubled between 1605 and 1661; it handled the bulk of English trade; its capital reached out to control provincial

13

economic development. Seat of court and government, centre of trade and law, London exercised a dominance that was, as Christopher Hill has said, 'unique in Europe' (**10**).

The prosperity of the city was not shared by all its inhabitants: the master-craftsman was a victim of the new capitalist age. Previously the small master had bought his own raw materials, worked on them, and sold them to the consumer; increasingly he now exercised his skills for an enterpreneur. He sold his labour; he was a wage-earner. Here was a major change in industrial organisation and one not readily accepted by the formerly independent master. It was possible, of course, to go up rather than down. Hard work, enterprise, or simple good luck might carry a craftsman off the workshop floor and into the capitalist class; a loan might save him, though interest rates were high and it was more likely to take him to a debtors' prison. But, in general, the craftsman was being depressed. Many apprentices would never become 'masters' at all; already there was a large class of journeymen who had long ago despaired of ever having an establishment of their own. Moreover, these men often came from a prosperous background— apprentice weavers had to be sons of freeholders owning an annual value of 40s a year—and they were bitterly mortified to find themselves descending the social scale; a slide often reflected by a move from the streets of the City to the suburbs of Southwark and Bermondsey across the Thames (**13**).

The guilds, of which they were still members, did nothing to help; rather the reverse, for in most cases all power within the guild had devolved upon the successful entrepreneur class. So the machinery which had in the Middle Ages been designed to ensure equality of rights and opportunities to its membership now reinforced the influence of those who flourished, at the expense of those who did not. Closely connected with this grievance was the problem of the government of London itself. In theory, it was controlled by the Court of Common Council, a body elected by all freemen of the City. In practice, the same forces had been at work as in the guilds and a narrow oligarchy of wealthy merchants monopolised power. As the Levellers' constitutional programme developed, it is clear that the artisans of London thought as much of their exclusion from the government of their own city as they did of the wider national issues. It was these men—the pewterers, weavers, cobblers, saddlers, clockmakers and other small tradesmen—who formed the main body of Leveller support. These were the ones John Lilburne spoke of when he described his supporters as 'the middle sort of people'. Independent of spirit, probably of above average intelligence, and likely to have taken advantage of recent advances in education (**41**), they were far more dangerous than the proletariat, which showed little interest in Leveller schemes.

The stresses within society brought about by the declining fortunes of copyholders and craftsmen were the result of basic structural changes within agriculture and industry. Between 1646 and 1649, however, these tensions were brought into high relief by the more normal uncertainties of war and nature. In 1646 there began a series of poor harvests that had a catastrophic effect on food prices. The price of bread more than doubled in a short time; oats, rye, peas and beans rose in proportion. The plight of the thousands who always lived on or near subsistence level was doleful. Despatches in the Leveller newspaper, *The Moderate*, spoke of near famine in places as far apart as Colchester and Lancaster; in Cumberland many 'died in the highways for lack of bread'. Although from a partial source not anxious to understate the sufferings of the poor, these reports need not be doubted. The unstable political conditions aggravated an already difficult situation. Wages failed to rise and unemployment was widespread; those who might have given employment preferred to conserve their resources for better times. Parliament, sadly short of funds, continued its excise, which covered many goods, including food and drink. 'The many thousand poor tradesmen' of London, whose 'mournful cries' were publicised in a Leveller pamphlet of January 1648, claimed they were destitute because no one could afford to buy their goods [**doc. 8**). There was genuine hardship in these years, hardship that provided the grass roots of the Leveller movement.

These privations were, as we have seen, countrywide, but it was in London that they merged with virulent Puritanism. London had long been the centre of opposition to the Anglican Church. Based primarily on a few parishes that had the right to appoint their own clergy, Puritanism had steadily gathered momentum under the first two Stuarts. Sermons and lectures by popular preachers were attended by large crowds; the punishment of Prynne, Bastwick and Burton in 1637 for their attacks on the bishops took place before an audience that was plainly sympathetic to the sufferers. Already industrial suburbs like Southwark, Wapping,

Blackfriars and Whitefriars had gained something of a reputation for extremism (**11**). When the episcopal censorship was abolished in 1641, these areas soon showed themselves susceptible to the more radical preachers. Here religious, social and economic discontent fused to form a dangerous harmony, which, with dedicated leadership and political opportunity, was destined to play a major part in the English Revolution.

3 The Political Scene

PARLIAMENT AND THE WESTMINSTER ASSEMBLY

The Long Parliament that met in 1640 and went to war with the king in 1642 reflected the patriarchal rule which nobles and gentry exercised over the countryside. Both Lords and Commons represented the propertied classes, with the landed interest pre-eminent. The mercantile element was also present, of course, though its extent is more difficult to estimate. There were, perhaps, fifty merchants in the original Commons, but this is hardly an accurate gauge of the trading influence; many of the gentry had invested in trade and industry, or were closely linked with the commercial world by marriage.

The franchise system ensured that the propertied classes maintained a firm grip on their position. In the county seats—the most socially desirable—the forty-shilling freeholder had the vote. The inflation had increased the number of such voters, but the majority were small men who dared not flout the wishes of larger local landowners; if simple respect born of social and economic inferiority did not produce the desired result, bribery and intimidation lay in reserve. In some counties the more distinguished families occupied a seat generation after generation and regarded it almost as hereditary property. The borough franchise was more complex, but here also it tended to be restricted to a small propertied minority, and again local landowners had the predominant influence. Both in counties and in boroughs the gentry bargained among themselves for the privilege of going to Westminster; some seats were bought and sold, others were fiercely contested, with parochial rivalries often more important than national ones. In both Houses a network of family relationships stretched across the benches; Oliver Cromwell, for example, had eighteen relations in the Commons. When the Levellers fell out with Parliament, they had little difficulty in persuading themselves that this select gathering was in no way representative of the population as a whole.

17

The Background

Yet in 1640, in spite of the narrow process of selection, parliament was, as far as can be seen, a fair reflection of opinion in the country at large. This was particularly true in the religious field where the destruction of the Laudian system met with wide approval. Under the tolerant eye of Laud's predecessor, Archbishop Abbot, Puritanism had made a steady advance. Puritan preachers had been presented to livings by sympathetic peers or gentry; others had been provided with lectureships by wealthy merchants or town corporations; yet others were installed as ministers by the Feoffees for Impropriations, a London group which bought up advowsons. Apart from a few separatists who had broken away, the main body of Puritans remained within the Church and their hope of an internal reformation did not seem impossible. Laud's appointment to Canterbury in 1633, however, threatened everything they had achieved. He enforced the rituals they loathed and which, in many cases, they had been ignoring; he suppressed lecturers and the Feoffees; he ordered preachers not to touch on controversial subjects; and he tightened up on censorship, vigorously punishing those, like Bastwick, Prynne and Burton, who were unwise enough to publish illicit pamphlets.

Laud's Arminianism gave the different strands of Puritanism a unity they had rarely achieved before and never experienced again. Together they turned on the bishops. They received support from another direction. Laud's activities not only offended theologically committed Puritans; many laymen were alienated by his attempts to recover impropriations and to re-rate tithes, which had dropped in value during the inflation. As a result, when Parliament met there were few prepared to give the bishops much support. Lord Falkland 'was wont to say that they who hated bishops hated them worse than the devil, and that they who loved them did not love them so well as their dinner'. The pent-up hostility of the 1630s, focused in the Long Parliament, destroyed the Courts of Star Chamber and High Commission, the main organs through which Laud had maintained discipline, and swept the archbishop himself into the Tower.

With all restraints removed, Puritan preachers sprang to their pulpits; pamphlets circulated freely; petitions were organised for presentation to parliament. This last development is important: the petition was a means of propaganda, involving a considerable degree of organisation, and was an effective means of bringing public opinion to bear on parliament. The Levellers were later to use it with great skill and must have learned many lessons during these early days when City M.P.s were in close touch with agitators in the streets. One such petition formed a prologue to the Puritan split that was shortly to appear. Presented in December 1640, it begged for the destruction of the existing church organisation 'roots and branches'; archbishops, bishops, deans, archdeacons—all were to be overthrown, to be replaced by 'the government according to God's Word'. At the time of its presentation, the Commons were more concerned with the immediate problem of getting rid of Strafford, but its proposals were embodied in the Bill debated in 1641 which became one of the links in the chain of events that led to the war itself.

Once Strafford, Laud, and the machinery of prerogative government had been removed, the opposition lost its sense of common purpose. Some were prepared to accept the traditional episcopalian organisation of the Church if it could be entrusted to safe hands, but a more radical, and more numerous, group supported the Root and Branch Bill. This division was reinforced by events outside the House. The disturbances in London during the Christmas of 1641 frightened the moderates. Craftsmen and apprentices were already involved in the frequent affrays that marked the mounting politico-religious tension. There were outbursts of iconoclasm and anticlericalism: the cross at Cheapside and the organ of St Paul's were defaced; several priests had their surplices torn from their backs; the Bishop of Chichester was greeted with cries of 'A Pope, a Pope!' when he preached at St Olave's, Old Jewry (48). Sectarian preachers had been among the first to take advantage of the freedom of the pulpit; cobblers, weavers and other manual workers harangued the crowds, claiming divine inspiration and pointing various paths to heaven. The more conservative members of the Commons sensed the danger of social revolt behind the excesses being perpetrated in the name of religious freedom. Sir John Strangeways, speaking in the debate on the Root and Branch petition, said: 'If we make a parity in the Church we must come to a parity in the Commonwealth'. (48). These stirrings of popular discontent and the pressure of the Root-and-Branchers go a long way to explain the growth of a royalist party in the Commons and the country at large.

The war broke out in 1642 with the whole religious question undecided. The extremists had their way in that bishops, deans and chapters were abolished by parliamentary ordinance, but it was one thing to destroy, quite another to reconstruct, and no authority was set up in their place to proclaim a new orthodoxy or to curb the antics of the 'mechanic preachers'. Eventually, in 1643, parliament called the Westminster Assembly into being to reconstitute the Church. It consisted of representatives of both houses of parliament, Puritan divines, and eight Scottish commissioners, who hoped to assist at the birth of a full Presbyterian system. At the same time, by the Solemn League and Covenant, parliament concluded a treaty with the Scots whereby the latter provided an army to fight the king, while parliament pledged 'the reformation of religion in the kingdoms of England and Ireland, in doctrine, worship, discipline and government, according to the Word of God, and the example of the best reformed churches'. In the course of the debates in the Westminster Assembly, the process of fission within Puritanism continued with a sharp disagreement over the exact nature of such a 'reformation'. The Root-and-Branchers fell out among themselves (**19**).

The main division was between Presbyterians and Independents. The former wanted a disciplined and comprehensive Presbyterian system—albeit an Erastian one—complete with presbyteries, regional synods and general assembly. The Independents, on the other hand, were suspicious of this authoritarian organisation. During Laud's régime, independent 'gathered' congregations had formed about individual Puritan preachers. They were not separatists but had followed a Puritan line within the Church when it had been difficult to do so. Having thrown off the shackles imposed by the bishops, they were not anxious to submit themselves to the rigid direction of a new central authority. They were willing to accept a national church as long as different congregations maintained some freedom within it; their demand was, in fact, for a measure of toleration.

The inherent contradictions of Calvinism here faced each other. The Presbyterians pointed to the heresies being propagated because of lack of discipline; the Independents insisted on the rights of the individual seeking his God. The Presbyterians, with a majority in the Assembly and the Commons, eventually succeeded in having an Erastian form of Presbyterianism established. But, thanks to lengthy filibustering by the Independents, this did not finally take place until 1646, by which time it was too late. Parliament was no onger in a position to enforce a strict religious settlement and the controversy over toleration had become involved with wider political and constitutional issues. The very titles 'Presbyterian' and 'Independent' had lost their clarity of definition.

While the Assembly had been discussing the religious settlement, a split had developed within the parliamentary camp over the more immediate problem of the prosecution of the war. A conservative group, tending to contain men of higher social status like the earls of Manchester and Essex, wanted a defensive war and a compromise peace with the king; it was opposed by a 'win-the-war' party, composed of those like Cromwell who felt that an outright victory was essential. The recriminations exchanged by the two sides, embittered by personal antagonism between Manchester and Cromwell, moved to a crisis in 1644 with the failure of the parliamentary armies to take advantage of their notable success at Marston Moor. Instead of seizing the initiative, they suffered a series of setbacks that made the end of the war seem as far away as ever. Waller's army mutinied after the engagement at Cropredy Bridge; Essex left his infantry to surrender at Lostwithiel following an ill-judged foray into Cornwall; and Manchester's pusillanimous conduct at the second battle of Newbury prevented a decisive victory. The result was a head-on clash in parliament in which the enthusiasts won the day. The New Model Army was created and the Self-denying Ordinance passed; the conservative generals had been forced out of the saddle and the way was clear for a coordinated campaign directed by men who believed in their cause. In this political field, the moderates who wanted 'an accommodation with His Majesty' were the 'Presbyterians' and the war party the 'Independents'.

Something more must be said about the terms 'Presbyterian' and 'Independent'. Historians are still divided over the beliefs and backgrounds of the men who sailed under these colours (**30**). Originally labels attached to those who disagreed over Church government, they came to be used in a political sense and the value of the religious definition deteriorated. One thing is clear from the confusion: it is very difficult to use the titles 'Presbyterian' and 'Independent' to distinguish continuous parties adhering to fixed principles. Like the terms Whig and Tory, they 'have been shown to be applicable to individuals only with respect to certain issues at certain specific times' (**37**). Experiences changed attitudes; groups coalesced and disintegrated in response to the constantly shifting panorama of

21

events they saw around them. The names Presbyterian and Independent will be used here, but it is to be understood that they refer to men adopting attitudes to particular problems, sometimes religious, sometimes political. To generalise, as one must if there is to be any clarity at all, the Presbyterians were on the side of conservatism and order, while the Independents were prepared to be more radical and wanted religious toleration.

Early in 1646 the royalist armies collapsed and their remaining garrisons surrendered. But the defeat of the king posed more problems than it solved. Parliament discovered that the army it had created had a will of its own and intended to keep a shrewd eye on the constitutional and religious settlement its victories had made possible. Parliament itself lacked real unity and was woefully short of money. The king added to the confusion, hoping to regain by tortuous negotiation that which he had lost in fair fight. There followed the most critical period of the whole century, in which left and right struggled for control of the revolution: the years that saw the rise and fall of the Leveller party.

THE ARMY

By 1645 it was clear that victory in the Civil War would go to the side that could first organise an efficient professional army. For three years decentralised armies had wandered over the countryside in desultory fashion, fighting battles giving a temporary local predominance but lacking qualities of real decision. Discipline was slack, money was short, and neither side had any systematic plan for making up the losses that followed a campaign. As a result, desertion was frequent, armies were never up to strength, and victories were frittered away; even the advantages gained for Parliament at Marston Moor were dissipated by the timid and inept generalship that followed. As one parliamentarian said in 1644: 'Our victories . . . seem to have been put in a bag with holes; what we won one time, we lost another' (**43**). It was this atmosphere of futility that led Cromwell, together with other officers like Waller and Massey, to press for a thorough overhaul of the parliamentary forces. The formation of the New Model Army and the passage of the Self-denying Ordinance marked their success. Naseby followed and by 1646 the war was won.

The original New Model consisted of eleven calvary regiments, twelve regiments of infantry, and one of dragoons; a combined total of 22,000 men. Sir Thomas Fairfax was appointed commander-in-chief with power to choose his own officers, subject only to parliamentary approval. Second in command was Oliver Cromwell, who bore the rank of lieutenant-general and led the cavalry; his able subordinate was Henry Ireton, chosen commissary-general of horse at Naseby. In charge of the infantry was Major-General Skippon, sometime commander of the London trained bands, an officer who had risen from the ranks and whose experience was invaluable in the early days when the army was being moulded into an effective fighting force. These men, backed by regimental commanders selected for their professional skill and devotion to the cause, formed a team the royalists could not match. In his *Memoirs*, Denzil Holles, leader of the Presbyterian party in the Commons and no friend to the New Model, spoke slightingly of the social background of its officers, claiming that most of them were 'mean tradesmen, brewers, tailors, goldsmiths, shoemakers and the like'. This calculated sneer may have been true of some of the junior officers, but it was without foundation with regard to the colonels and senior commanders. Of thirty-seven leading officers, nine came from noble families and only seven were not 'gentlemen'. Certainly they were men of a calibre that boded ill to politicians who might imagine their wishes could be flouted once the war was over (**43**).

The army did not earn its reputation overnight. Contemporaries regarded it with scepticism. Robert Baillie, one of the Scottish commissioners in London, wrote: 'Their new-modelled army consists, for the most, of raw, unexperienced, pressed soldiers. Few of the officers are thought capable of their places . . . if they do great things, many will be deceived.' This was an exaggeration, but rather more than half the infantry were pressed men whose zeal was seriously in doubt; initially they deserted in droves and Fairfax complained that he had not half the number of foot he ought to have had under the establishment. Nevertheless, in spite of the moans of the fainthearts and the ill-disguised hopes of those who had suffered in the reorganisation, the New Model steadily built up its numbers and, more important, developed an *esprit de corps* almost wholly lacking in previous parliamentary armies.

It had certain obvious advantages. In the first place, it was a national army prepared to fight anywhere, not merely a local levy

whose interest began and ended at home. It was under the central
direction of an all-powerful commander-in-chief who soon freed
himself from the inhibiting control of the Committee of Both
Kingdoms when it tried to dictate strategy to him. Without going
as far as the late H. N. Brailsford, who called it a 'People's Army' in
which 'there can have been no class barrier between officers and
men' (**13**), it may be said that promotion went largely on merit
and it was perfectly possible for a man of ability to rise from the
ranks. Furthermore, its discipline was good. From the opening of his
first campaign, when he had two men hanged for plundering,
Fairfax made it plain that his soldiers were not going to disgrace
themselves with the disorders that had marked the passage of earlier
parliamentary armies.

The cavalry were the *élite* of the army. They were usually of higher
social class than the infantry, being men of small independent
means—often yeomen and craftsmen—men likely to be 'of good
parts and learning'. Most recruits brought their own horses and
arms and all were volunteers. Just as they were the aggressive arm
in battle, so the cavalry took the lead in the political disturbances of
1647. Despite the increasing tactical importance of the infantry with
the development of firearms, the foot soldier remained the poor
relation. His pay, eightpence a day, had not risen since the reign
of Elizabeth and even this meagre sum was reduced by deductions
for uniform and billet. It is small wonder that the press gang had
to work hard to fill the ranks. The custom of impressment was one
of the first military grievances to be exploited by the Levellers
[**doc. 5**].

The war must have done much to change the outlook of those
who became soldiers, whether cavalry or infantry. Taken out of their
narrow village or town environment and shown a wider national
perspective, they experienced more in the concentrated excitement
of a few years than most of their ancestors did in a lifetime. Moreover, the hurly-burly of battle, in which all were equal in the
struggle for survival, must have done much to diminish their sense
of social inferiority. Previously the sword had been the prerogative
of the 'gentlemen'; now it was worn by all. This emancipation from
the psychological burden of being one of the lower degrees in the
social hierarchy was symbolised by the eventual execution of the
king. It took considerable courage to shatter the mystique of
monarchy with one formal blow; such courage was forged in the

heat of the Civil War when the preordained order of things so often seemed to be turned upside down (**39**).

One of the most notable characteristics of the New Model was the intensity of its religious feeling. The pressed men of the infantry in all probability had few religious beliefs—indeed one regiment of foot mutinied when an officer tried to preach to them—but many of the remainder, particularly in the cavalry, were strongly imbued with Puritanism. Cromwell himself is the best example of the soldier convinced that he was fighting for God's cause. An Independent who believed that 'the Kingdom of God is within us', he saw all his military successes as confirmation of divine inspiration and support. 'God made them stubble to our swords', he wrote after Marston Moor; 'This is none other than the hand of God', after Naseby; 'The Lord hath showed us an exceeding mercy', after Dunbar. This massive confidence in the favour of Providence was shared by many of his men, notably by the erstwhile troops of the Eastern Association who had been incorporated into the New Model. William Dell, an army chaplain, found more signs of godliness in the army than among any other group of people he had met before, and even royalists commented favourably on its piety and sobriety. The popular vision of psalm-singing Ironsides is well founded in fact (**43, 44**).

The Puritanism that flourished in the army did not follow conventional Presbyterian teaching. At the opening of the war, a number of Presbyterian chaplains were attached to Essex's army, but after Edgehill many of these retired from the rigours of military life, taking over livings vacated by episcopalians. As a result, the spread of unorthodox opinions went unchecked and within two years of its foundation the New Model was dominated by the Independents. Of these, some followed the line of the Independents in the Westminster Assembly and simply wanted a degree of toleration; others were already forming separatist sects that had no time for a national church at all. Together they found coherence in opposition to the parliamentary attempt to set up an authoritarian Presbyterian system.

The growth of Independency was fostered by the army chaplains—men like William Dell, Hugh Peters and John Saltmarsh—whose advanced views horrified traditionalist Presbyterians. Richard Baxter was so shocked when he visited the New Model in 1645 that he stayed on as a chaplain for a while in an endeavour to counter the heretical ideas permeating its ranks. Everywhere he found talk of liberty of conscience and demands 'that every man might not only hold, but preach and do in matters of religion what he pleased'. Although there was a parliamentary order forbidding lay preaching, it was virtually ignored by officers and men. The army had become a forum for the free discussion of religious ideas, ideas frequently leading to the extreme individualist position of free will and universal grace. Given the right circumstances, it was but a short step from the demand for religious freedom to the demand for political freedom also. Such circumstances were soon to be forthcoming.

Relations between parliament and the army had not been perfect even during the war. The natural friction between soldiers and civilians had been exacerbated by a new press censorship, the attempts to limit preaching, and, above all, by parliament's failure to keep pay up to date. This latent antagonism came to a head in the spring of 1647 when the Presbyterian majority in parliament, anxious for a speedy return to the stable conditions of a well ordered state and highly suspicious of the rampant Independency among the troops, determined to disband part of the New Model and send the remainder to Ireland. Unfortunately, in its haste to eliminate a contender for power in the political vacuum that followed the defeat of the king, parliament showed little acumen or imagination. By March 1647 army pay had fallen sadly into arrears; the infantry were owed eighteen weeks, the cavalry forty-three. The plans for demobilisation gave no guarantees for these arrears. Nor did they provide legal indemnity to save soldiers from peace-time prosecution for acts committed during the war. Moreover, the proposed army for Ireland was to be an entirely new formation and the services of Independent officers, like Cromwell, were to be dispensed with. These affronts put the army in a dangerous mood: here was the Levellers' opportunity.

LEVELLER POLITICS

So far we have seen certain forces—Puritanism, social and economic discontent, and the development of an unstable politico-religious situation—producing conditions in which a revolutionary movement might flourish. It would be a sad mistake, however, to explain the emergence of the Levellers as the simple workings of historical determinism. Indeed, few political movements have been so dependent on the personalities of their leaders and it is essential to say something of the characters and early careers of these men if the Levellers are to be understood.

Four men were mainly responsible for directing Leveller fortunes: John Lilburne, William Walwyn, Richard Overton and John Wildman. Others, like Thomas Rainsborough and Edward Sexby, played vital roles at particular times, and there must have been many smaller figures toiling in the depths of the party machinery in London whose names have not survived. But these four bore the heat of the day. Diverse in character and beliefs, yet strangely complementary to each other, they provided the vision and energy that helped to keep the revolution moving towards the left between 1647 and 1649 and for a short while threatened to seize control of it altogether.

John Lilburne

At first glance, Lilburne is not an attractive figure. Obstinate, extrovert, arrogantly refusing to bow to any form of authority, he was a supreme egotist with an exaggerated sense of his own grievances. Lacking in humour and quick to take offence on his own and other people's behalf, he looks like a barrackroom lawyer of the worst type. One contemporary critic described him as 'never well but when fishing in troubled waters . . . a busy body meddling with other men's matters'. More succinctly, the royalist weekly, *Mercurius Pragmaticus*, designated him the 'lunatic Lieutenant Colonel'.

Yet this is a good deal less than half the picture. Certainly he was a born rebel, but his was not the narrow, prejudiced revolt of the man with a chip on his shoulder. He had a passionate hatred of injustice of any sort and his whole life was dedicated to the ideal of freedom in its widest sense. Willing to suffer any hardship if the cause was right, he constantly lashed out at the strong to protect the weak. His generosity of spirit embraced anyone with a real grievance; characteristically, he was as forward in demanding justice for defeated royalists as he was for himself. His genius for putting his own wrongs at the centre of a conflict of principle was something more than mere exhibitionism. As champion of the oppressed, he felt it his duty to resist illegality at every turn, for 'what is done to anyone may be done to everyone'. For fulfilling his duty to his fellow men he was flogged, gaoled over and over again, and tried three times for his life. His turbulent career, in which comedy and tragedy are never far apart, is at all times worthy of respect.

Lilburne was the natural leader of the Levellers. Energetic, determined, and exuding considerable personal charm, he had no difficulty in collecting supporters and holding them together. His pamphlets tended to be rambling and shapeless, but none could miss their burning conviction, and every now and then he hit on a pithy phrase that went to the heart of the matter. His defiance of authority was linked with a flair for propaganda and publicity. Whether making an impromptu speech from the pillory in New Palace Yard or refusing to remove his hat at the bar of the House of Lords, he was aware of the image he was creating: 'Free-born John', martyr in the cause of the downtrodden. This was an appealing picture that crystallised all the hopes and fears of the small men of London and brought them crowding to his assistance.

Lilburne was a gentleman by birth—as he pointed out more than once—coming from a family of small landowners in County Durham. Being a younger son, he was, in 1630, apprenticed to a Puritan cloth merchant in London. It is difficult to overestimate the importance of these early years in the development of his character. As an impressionable and rather gauche young man, he was plunged into a city strong in Puritanism and soon to be seething with hostility to Laud's Arminian régime. He read voraciously— the Bible, history, law, a multitude of books on Puritan theology, and anything else he could lay his hands on; he discussed religion with other apprentices and imbibed all the Puritan influences around him. He was soon introduced to John Bastwick and William Prynne, who currently held the stage as Laud's most outspoken opponents. It was this relationship that led Lilburne to his first martyrdom.

In December 1637 Lilburne, now aged twenty-two, was arrested and charged with having smuggled an antiprelatical pamphlet by Bastwick from Holland. Taken before Star Chamber, he gave evasive answers to all questions, would not pay the clerk's fee, and then became the first man to refuse the notorious *ex officio* oath in that court. His accusers lost patience and sentenced him to be flogged, pilloried, and imprisoned indefinitely. This punishment played right into the hands of one who was determined to emulate his heroes in Foxe's *Book of Martyrs*. While being 'smartly whipped from the Fleet to Westminster', he recited the Scriptures and cried out 'Hallelujah! Hallelujah!'; at the pillory he made an impromptu speech until he was gagged, at which point he scattered leaflets from his pockets; his return to prison was something of a triumphal procession with enthusiastic admirers providing an escort.

Back in the Fleet, covered in weals 'bigger than tobacco-pipes' and shackled in irons by special order of the Star Chamber, Lilburne experienced an ecstatic spiritual revelation that gave him the certainty of salvation and transformed his life. He now knew himself to be one of God's chosen instruments, one of the elect assured of an 'immortal Crown'. From now on his natural anger at injustice was to be purified and transmuted by his deep religious faith; his intractable, uncompromising character was fused with a white-hot Puritan fanaticism. As he wrote shortly after his ordeal: 'I honour and glorify my God, who hath passed by so many thousands as he hath done, and left them in their sins, and yet hath chosen me freely before the foundation of the world was laid'. There was all the confidence and arrogance of a man who could lead a revolution.

Released from prison in 1640 after a speech on his behalf by Oliver Cromwell, Lilburne, with the help of his prosperous uncle George of Sunderland, set himself up as a brewer and got married. He was prominent in the disturbances at Westminster in December 1641 and joined the parliamentary army as a captain in Lord Brooke's regiment at the outbreak of war. He fought at Edgehill and later distinguished himself in the engagement at Brentford, where he was taken prisoner. After rejecting bribes to get him to change sides, he found himself charged with treason and on trial for his life at Oxford. His conduct at the trial followed the extravagant pattern of exhibitionism that marked his frequent appearances in the dock. Claiming that he was a gentleman, he refused to plead to an indictment calling him a yeoman; later he offered to fight any two of his accusers single-handed. Not surprisingly the court declared, 'This fellow is mad.' Mad or not, he would almost certainly have been hanged had it not been for the courage of his wife, who petitioned parliament for help. She herself took the Commons' threat of retaliation on royalists to Oxford and helped to arrange the exchange of prisoners that freed her husband.

Back in the parliamentary army, Lilburne joined a regiment of foot in the Eastern Association. Inevitably trouble followed. He played an important part in the cashiering of his own commanding officer for incompetence and shortly after this fell foul of the Earl of Manchester, thus helping to highlight the growing split between enthusiastic Independents and dilatory Presbyterians. To the fury of Manchester, who threatened to hang him, he captured the royalist castle of Tickhill in defiance of orders. He wanted to resign immediately after this, but stayed on to please Cromwell, with whom he had become friendly and who wanted to use Lilburne in his political campaign against Manchester and the fainthearts.

At the creation of the New Model, Lilburne gave up his commission because he would not take the oath to the Solemn League and Covenant which was a precondition of service in the new formation. Many Independents (in the religious sense), including Cromwell, had qualms of conscience about this but were prepared to compromise. Lilburne was not, and his return to civilian life in 1645 marks his deviation from the mainstream of Calvinist thought. From this point on he became a potent ally of those like Walwyn and Overton who had already joined battle with the Presbyterians over the issue of religious toleration (**47, 48**).

William Walwyn

William Walwyn was born in 1600, the second son of a well-to-do landowner in Worcestershire; his maternal grandfather was the Bishop of Hereford. Apprenticed in London, he became a member of the Merchant Adventurers Company early in the 1630s and was soon a prosperous merchant. His family life seems to have been extremely happy, though whether because of, or despite, 'almost twenty children' borne by his wife it is hard to say. It would be difficult to imagine a greater contrast than that between Lilburne and Walwyn. The former relished the limelight and publicised every moment of his stormy career; Walwyn remains a veiled figure moving in the shadows, a self-effacing enigma the extent of whose influence is doubtful. In fact, so far as one may tell, he was the dominant intellectual force in the Leveller movement.

Walwyn is the most immediately attractive of the Levellers. Good-natured, tolerant, a lover of his library and garden, he seems curiously out of place in the maelstrom of contemporary political life; his pamphlets were usually marked by a kindly humour and never sank to the bitter vituperation that informed the works of both his friends and enemies. He read widely, including Plutarch,

Seneca and Montaigne as well as the Bible and works of Puritan theology more acceptable to his day and age. His intellectual development was calm and unhurried, more in sympathy with the rational humanism of the Renaissance than the fierce intolerance engendered by the Reformation. One feature of his thought ties him very closely to the Renaissance indeed. The classical idea of a state of nature, a Golden Age when men held all things in common and had no need of government at all, made a strong appeal to him. It led to a dislike of anything artificial leading man away from his primitive past towards a sophisticated society. More important, the idealised state of nature, in which all took enough for his needs and no more, gave him a yardstick with which to judge the imperfections of the world he saw around him. It reinforced the conclusions he reached via his own particular type of Puritanism.

Walwyn was an intensely religious man and only an understanding of his beliefs can lead to a grasp of the social and political theories he felt bound to advance as the revolution worked itself out. He approached the Bible with humility, yet in a spirit of rational enquiry. Some time before 1640 the apparent contradictions he discovered there brought on a deep spiritual crisis. Quite apart from the questions of his own salvation, he was perplexed by the fact that a good God had seemingly consigned millions of unfortunates to everlasting hell: a dilemma reflected in the Bible by the conflict between the law of the Old Testament and the grace offered by the New. Eventually, Walwyn's answer to this problem was simple, logical, and characteristic of the generous mind that produced it. Man, he knew, was sinful and deserved the pains of damnation. But God, being a God of love, offered salvation through Christ, salvation not merely for a small coterie of saints, as the Calvinist dogmatists would have it, but to all men prepared to make the effort to accept it. He wrote: 'Ye are all justified freely by his grace through the redemption that is in Jesus Christ.'

Having used his own powers of reason to emancipate himself from rigid dogma, Walwyn naturally became an advocate of religious toleration for all—a toleration he wanted to extend to the hated Roman Catholics as well as the Puritan sects. 'Of all liberty,' he wrote, 'liberty of conscience is the greatest.' Most Independents saw, in Milton's words, that new Presbyter was but old Priest writ large, and none saw it more clearly than Walwyn, who had found his own faith unaided by the ministerial caste and was deeply suspicious of all who stood in pulpits claiming a monopoly of the truth and confounding ordinary men with the subtlety of their theology. The truth was simple, to be discovered by the individual in the Scriptures, 'the only true infallible teacher of spiritual things in our time'.

All Walwyn's early pamphlets had religious toleration as the main subject, and it was this struggle for freedom of conscience that first drew the future Leveller leaders together. But there were soon signs of Walwyn applying his religious beliefs to more secular problems. His pamphlet *The Power of Love*, published in 1643, shows important links between Puritan theology and the demand for social reform. God's love for men, he argued, should be reflected in love between men—a love that should manifest itself in the betterment of the condition of those who were poor:

> He that hath this world's goods, and seeth his brother lack, how dwelleth the love of God in him? . . . Look about you and you will find in these woeful days thousands of miserable, distressed, starved, imprisoned Christians: see how pale and wan they look: how coldly, raggedly, and unwholesomely they are clothed . . . then walk abroad, and observe the general plenty of all necessaries, observe the gallant bravery of multitudes of men and women abounding in all things that can be imagined: observe likewise the innumerable numbers of these that have more than sufficeth (**14**).

This is more than an exhortation to traditional Christian charity. The condemnation of economic inequality is already implicit; soon it was to become the dominant theme of his work (**14, 26**).

Richard Overton

The third member of the quartet, Richard Overton, was a man of whose background little is known. Early in the century he separated from the Anglican Church and joined a sect of English Baptists in Amsterdam. These were in communion with a branch of Dutch Mennonites and Overton thus provides the strongest Leveller connexion with continental Anabaptism. From this source he gained his belief in religious toleration and the separation of church and state. He was back in England by 1641, operating an unlicensed printing press, and in 1642 he published two satirical poems attacking the remnants of Roman Catholicism and the fallen Laud.

Overton lacked the polish and equable temper of Walwyn. He was altogether blunter and his sense of humour was more rough-hewn. In his Martin Marpriest tracts, based on the Elizabethan Martin Marprelate and published in 1645 when the fight for religious freedom was reaching a climax, he relished the medieval tradition of anticlericalism, lampooning the Presbyterian divines as the 'brisk and spermatick sons of the bishops' who had a 'godly care for their own guts'. Though probably of a lower social class than either Lilburne or Walwyn, he seems to have received quite a good education and his pamphlets reflect the workings of a disciplined mind.

Overton first gained notoriety as a daring free-thinker in 1644 when he published *Man's Mortality*, a heretical work that shocked many Independents as well as Presbyterians. In it he argues that the idea of man's soul going to heaven or hell at death is 'a mere fiction'. When man dies, he dies completely; body and soul are one and subject to the same laws of nature; in this respect man is no different from an animal. To prove his case, he uses biblical quotations, biological analysis, and a materialistic mode of argument. He goes on to say that at the Resurrection both body and soul will rise to immortality. Although Overton made obeisance to this final miracle, he was attacked as an atheist and some historians have suggested that this addition was made simply to avoid the death penalty for unbelief. In fact, the idea of the death of the soul had long been current among central European Anabaptists and there is little reason to doubt Overton's basic Christianity. What is important about this pamphlet is not so much its content as the adventurous rationalism of Overton's thought, which, in spite of his traditional use of scriptural texts, presaged the materialism of the Levellers when they emerged as a coherent political party (**13, 14**).

John Wildman

John Wildman was the odd man out. He came late to the Leveller movement and left early; he was the only one of the four leaders who was not a religious man. Not for him the blinding emotional revelation of Lilburne or the tortured doubts of Walwyn. Contemporaries described him variously as an Anabaptist, a Fifth Monarchist and a Quaker, but, in fact, he was an agnostic whose religion was formal and perfunctory. Although prepared to use scriptural texts where they suited his purpose and because they were expected of him, he easily became exasperated by the bibliolatry of the Puritans and their constant seeking for divine guidance when faced with secular decisions. During the Putney debates, when Levellers and army officers were discussing constitutional proposals, he said bluntly: 'We cannot find anything in the Word of God what is fit to be done in civil matters.'

Nothing is known of Wildman's ancestry, but he was a 'gentleman' and married, in turn, the daughters of a Roman Catholic baronet and Lord Lovelace. Born in 1623, he is said to have been to Cambridge, though he does not appear to have graduated, and to have studied law in London. He was often referred to as Major Wildman, but his military career, if any, is obscure and he was without doubt a civilian when he took part in the Putney debates. Whatever his training, he had a reputation for his knowledge of the law and it was for his legal ability that he was valuable to the Levellers. It was he who drew up the first version of their proposed constitution, The Agreement of the People.

It is difficult to say what attracted Wildman towards Lilburne and his colleagues in the first place. It was certainly not religion. It may have been the republican theories the Levellers were beginning to develop, or it may simply have been Wildman's love of political intrigue. No one enjoyed shady backstairs plots more than he did; no one was more cautious or more secretive. He was, in the words of his biographer, Maurice Ashley, a 'professional conspirator', and his subsequent career gives some idea of his passion for plotting, as well as his talent for survival (**45**). He was involved in practically every conspiracy against Cromwell during the Protectorate, including Sindercombe's bizarre and abortive assassination attempts. He negotiated with the exiled royalists, though at this point he covered his tracks so successfully that it is hard to see how genuine his support was; he *may* have been acting as a double agent for Thurloe, Cromwell's secretary-of-state. In 1659 he took part in a plot aimed at putting Charles II's younger brother James on the throne. After the Restoration, he conspired intermittently against the Stuarts. Imprisoned for his share in the Rye House Plot, Wildman was forced to flee the country after complicity in Monmouth's rising; in exile, he busied himself with the schemes that culminated in the Revolution of 1688. At length, under William and Mary, he settled for respectability. He became for a short while postmaster-general, then deputy-lieutenant of Middlesex, and achieved a knighthood in 1692, shortly before his death.

Wildman lacked the dedication and consistency of his more religious comrades. In a sense he was not one of the true Leveller leaders, but he is included here because he was for a time a close friend of Lilburne and held an important position in the party during the most critical phase of its existence. Wildman genuinely wanted greater political liberty and he made a courageous stand against Cromwell at Putney, but it is difficult to avoid the conclusion that he revelled in legalistic dispute and was comparatively indifferent to the social and humanitarian implications within the Leveller programme. Indeed, soon after the defeat of the Levellers, he retired from the party, launched himself into land speculation on a large scale, and speedily amassed a considerable fortune. Richard Overton roundly condemned his desertion of the cause:

> And where's my old fellow rebel, Johnny Wildman? ... And behold a mighty stone fell from the skies into the bottom of the sea, and gave a mighty plump, and great was the fall of that stone, and so farewell, Johnny Wildman.'

To Overton, Wildman's defection was unpardonable. In fact, he had never been as committed to the ethos of the Leveller movement as his erstwhile colleagues and his falling-off, once the hope of success had gone, was in keeping with his inherent opportunism (**45**).

Part Two

ANALYSIS

4 The Rise and Fall of the Leveller Party

THE STRUGGLE FOR TOLERATION

From an early stage in the Civil War, the conservative Presbyterians recognised the dangers likely to follow the collapse of royal authority in Church and State. They were appalled by many of the ideas that circulated in sermons and pamphlets, and anxiously awaited the time when new disciplines could be set up on the ruins of the old. No real stability could return until the war had been won, but in the meanwhile the ground could be prepared. With a majority in parliament and the Westminster Assembly, the Presbyterians set about the task of erecting a system of Presbyterianism which would restrain the worst excesses of the sectaries and restore a sense of order.

In 1643 parliament reinstituted press censorship, ordering that no book was to be published without licence from the Stationers' Company and empowering the Parliamentary Committee of Examinations to search for illicit presses. The alliance with the Scots in the same year by the Solemn League and Covenant strengthened the Presbyterian hand, though the English Presbyterians in parliament had no intention of allowing their religious settlement to be anything other than Erastian. In January 1645 parliament accepted the Directory of Worship, as put forward by the Westminster Assembly, and in the months that followed provision was made for the establishment of intolerant Presbyterianism in London and throughout the country. This was the background for the battle over liberty of conscience that went on throughout the Civil War; a battle fought in the Westminster Assembly (where the delaying tactics of John Goodwin and the Independents were so successful that the eventual Presbyterian settlement was stillborn) in the pulpit and in the press [**doc. 1**]. It was into this struggle that the future Leveller leaders went individually; they emerged as a cohesive force.

Press censorship had not been effective under Laud and it was not so now. Quiet, reasonable and optimistic, Walwyn was one of the first to publish pamphlets advocating religious freedom and defending the rights of sectaries. Overton joined the assault on the Presbyterians with his robust Martin Marpriest tracts, holding up to ridicule the allegorical figures of Sir Simon Synod, Sir John Presbyter and Mr Persecution. The Presbyterians did not lack for champions in this vituperative pamphlet warfare. William Prynne, once an ally of Lilburne, had already come forward to defend orthodoxy. His bitter attacks on the Independents added a new dimension to the invective being hurled from side to side. Prynne's appearance in the lists stirred Lilburne himself to a stern denunciation of intolerance ('To persecute for conscience is not from God, but of and from the Devil and Antichrist') and, typically, to a challenge to Prynne to a public debate. The three chief Leveller leaders were thus committed to the cause of toleration. Furthermore, at some point in the summer of 1645 they had almost certainly met each other for the first time. Lilburne and Walwyn were taking part in political discussions at the Windmill Tavern, and the fact that parliament suspected Lilburne of responsibility for the Marpriest tracts suggests that he also knew Overton. By the end of the year, Lilburne and Overton were sharing the same secret press, run by one Larner.

In July 1645 Lilburne became the centre of a personal dispute which did much to shift his thinking, and that of his friends, from religious to political ground. Two of his enemies, the Presbyterian Bastwick, whose protégé he had once been, and Colonel King, for whose dismissal as commander of his regiment Lilburne had been partly responsible, jointly informed the Commons that Lilburne had said that its Speaker, William Lenthall, had sent £60,000 to the enemy at Oxford. In fact, Lilburne had merely been one of a group, which included the cavalry commander Henry Ireton, discussing certain information to be laid against Lenthall. Bastwick and King saw their chance of incriminating Lilburne and took it. He found himself arrested and taken before the Parliamentary Committee of Examinations on a charge of slandering the Speaker. Before the Committee Lilburne was as intractable as ever and likened its proceedings to those of Star Chamber. He refused to answer questions, challenged its right to act as a court at all, and read out extracts of Magna Carta to justify his demands for a fair trial. Committed to Newgate, he spent the three months before his release publicising his predicament and claiming martyrdom on behalf of all free-born Englishmen whose rights were endangered by the arbitrary processes he had undergone.

This was an illuminating episode in several ways. The Commons' handling of Lilburne was undoubtedly very highhanded and reflected the reactionary attitude of many of its members towards those known to be troublemakers on the left. This unexpected treatment by the body for which he had until recently been risking his life on the battlefield, forced Lilburne to clarify his own ideas on the relationship between the individual subject and Parliament. It led him to produce a statement which was to become the basic creed on which all future Leveller thinking was to be based:

> For my part, I look upon the House of Commons as the supreme power of England, who have residing in them that power that is inherent in the people, who yet are not to act according to their own wills and pleasure, but according to the fundamental constitutions and customs of the land, which I conceive provides for the safety and preservation of the people (**14**).

Moreover, his pamphlet *England's Birthright Justified,* written and printed while he was in Newgate, showed an increasing appreciation of social and economic issues. After his demand for the observance of the rule of law, he lashed out at many targets. Grasping lawyers operating incomprehensible laws written in Latin and French, tithes, the excise—'which lays the burden [of taxation] heavily on the poor, and men of middle quality or condition . . .'—the monopoly of the wealthy Merchant Adventurers—all came under fire. Although the main issue at stake between parliament and its critics was still religious toleration, it is clear that other antagonisms were not far beneath the surface and Lilburne was already offering a political manifesto in embryo.

Towards the end of the same year, Overton, seeking a new opening for an attack on the Presbyterians, took up the tithe grievance, already mentioned by Lilburne, and developed it in his Marpriest pamphlet *The Ordinance for Tithes Dismounted.* Tithes had always been hated and at a time of upheaval when the existence of all established institutions was being questioned it was inevitable that they should come to the fore. Opposition to tithes was based partly on the simple economic ground that no one liked paying out money, even if it did support a minister of God, and partly on the belief, not uncommon among the Independents, that the local minister should be maintained by the voluntary gifts of his congregation. It is a significant indication of the widespread hostility to tithes that their abolition became part of the programme of any group in the Civil War period hoping to broaden the basis of its popular support.

Two main dangers were seen by those who resisted any attempt to tamper with tithes. In the first place, it was realised by all who cherished the authority of Church and State that as a weapon of propaganda the pulpit was invaluable. Charles I, himself, said: 'People are governed by pulpits more than the sword in time of peace.' To allow control of the pulpit to fall into the hands of the congregation by putting the minister at the mercy of his flock for a stipend was to throw away an effective organ of government. The Presbyterians certainly had no intention of losing it and in 1644 Parliament passed an ordinance to enforce tithe payments to the new incumbents of livings sequestered from episcopalians. But there was another, more serious, danger seen by those who favoured the *status quo*. Many tithes did not go to the church at all, but to laymen —to 'impropriators', who had bought church lands from the crown after the Reformation. Thus there was a strong vested interest of landowners to resist any attempt to do away with tithes. And the link between tithes and property was closer than this. If tithes could be done away with, why should rents be sacrosanct? A petition against tithes presented to the Commons in 1646 already juxtaposed 'griping landlords' with tithe collectors (**40**).

So when Overton published *The Ordinance for Tithes Dismounted*, in which his main object was to pillory the greed of the persecuting Presbyterians, he was touching a very sensitive nerve indeed and one likely to confirm the Presbyterians in their innate conservatism. Once tithes were criticised, property rights were in danger and the whole fabric of society shook.

The following year, 1646, was distinguished by a notable pamphlet duel between Walwyn and a choleric Presbyterian minister, Thomas Edwards. The latter, in his diatribe *Gangraena*, urged parliament to more effective persecution of the heresies multiplying throughout the country. By giving precise details of the errors he had unearthed and showing how widespread they were, he hoped to shock parliament into action. He attacked individual preachers by name, vilified them with abuse, and garnished his accounts with descriptions of the many sexual and other misdemeanours to which they were naturally prone. Significantly, Edwards already treated Lilburne, Walwyn and Overton as a group and the venom he expends on them suggests that he anticipated special dangers from this direction. Walwyn's defence was superb and left him master of the field. Disdaining the crude polemics of his foe, he pricked the bubble of Edwards's anger with subtle irony. He feigned pity for the sad malady that afflicted Edwards, giving him so jaundiced and unchristian a view of life, and recommended as a remedy the application of a little love. 'Use inwardly and outwardly,' he advised, ' . . . and you will find your disposition to alter . . . until you come to be a strong and healthful Christian.' At the same time he continued to put forward a calmly reasoned case for liberty of conscience, pointing out that 'compulsion and enforcement may make a confused mass of dissembling hypocrites, not a congregation of believers'.

Lilburne was never far from the centre of the stage and in the summer of 1646 he became involved in a more serious wrangle with parliament. The origins of the dispute are complex, but they concerned both his demand for payment of arrears of army pay and compensation for his treatment by Star Chamber, as well as his personal vendetta with Colonel King. In the course of the row, Lilburne published his version of the matter and, in a typically provocative aside, made derogatory mention of the Presbyterian Earl of Manchester, now Speaker of the House of Lords. Lilburne was promptly arrested and taken before the bar of the Upper House. There his conduct was predictable: he defied the House in a series of dramatic scenes. He claimed that as he was a commoner the Lords had no jurisdiction over him—a claim he publicised in *The Free-man's Freedom Vindicated*; he refused to remove his hat or to kneel at the bar; when the charge against him was read out, he covered his ears. The Lords lost patience with him and passed a vicious sentence which once again gave Lilburne the crown of martyrdom. He was fined £2,000, forbidden to hold any military or civil office in the future, and condemned to close imprisonment in the Tower; to add insult to injury, his two offending pamphlets were to be burned by the common hangman.

Lilburne's punishment raised fundamental issues that had been foreshadowed by his earlier imprisonment by the Commons—

issues which were secular, not religious. And there were wider implications, as Lilburne showed in a speech he made to the Lords shortly before his sentence:

> All you intended when you set us a-fighting was merely to unhorse and dismount our old riders and tyrants, that so you might get up, and ride us in their stead. And therefore, my Lords . . . if you shall be so unworthy as to persevere . . . in the destruction of the fundamental laws and liberties of England . . . I will venture my life and heart's blood against you, with as much zeal and courage as ever I did against any of the King's party (**13**).

The disillusionment expressed here mirrored the feelings of many who, as the Civil War lay in its death throes, wondered just what they had been fighting to achieve. Here was a question mark over the whole revolution.

This new imprisonment, born of a clash between the growing nervousness of the conservatives and the erratic ebullience of the man already making a name as a leader of the demand for religious toleration, was to provide the focal point for the formation of the Leveller party.

THE BIRTH OF THE PARTY

In June 1646 the Civil War came to an end. The king surrendered to the Scots, and parliament set about the task of restoring some form of constitutional government. On the face of it, the problem was simple: parliament had defeated the king and might reasonably suppose that an agreement could be reached whereby its victory in war would be consolidated by a shift in the balance of power within the constitution. Neither Presbyterians nor Independents could as yet conceive of government without the king; Charles merely had to be persuaded that a new relationship had developed between Crown and Parliament and then all could return to normal. In fact the situation was a good deal more complicated than this. In the first place, a speedy, amicable settlement depended on Charles I's recognition of the change that had taken place in his position; this he consistently refused to do. He had no intention whatsoever of consenting to any diminution in his powers, or of accepting the Presbyterian Church; he was prepared to negotiate, but was only playing for time until the divisions he perceived amongst his enemies widened sufficiently for him to nullify the effects of the war and reach a settlement entirely satisfactory to himself. Moreover, although the Presbyterians had control of parliament, they were weak in the army and, however sanguine they might be, there was no guarantee that the Independent officers would accept any compromise which did not allow for their views. To confuse the issue further, the Scots, having helped to win the war, were not unwilling to have a hand in the peace and hoped the king might be induced to take the Covenant. The negotiations that followed provided the background for the emergence of the Levellers.

The title 'Leveller'—a term of abuse used by opponents—did not come into general use until late in 1647, but the most recent historian of the Levellers dates the birth of the party from the appearance of *A Remonstrance of many thousand citizens* . . ., a pamphlet written in the main by Overton and Walwyn and published a few days before the Lords' sentence on Lilburne (**13**). Taking Lilburne's tribulations as their starting point, the authors built up a comprehensive indictment of the existing Parliament and put forward revolutionary constitutional proposals for the future. Working from the basic premise that all power lies in the people, *A Remonstrance* demanded the abolition of the monarchy and, by implication, of the House of Lords. The tenor of the personal attack on Charles I— 'We do expect . . . that ye should . . . declare and set forth King Charles his wickedness openly before the world . . .'—already hinted at the later Leveller demand for his trial and punishment. The present House of Commons, castigated for its reactionary record, was to dissolve itself as soon as possible; to ensure that a new Commons should not in future ignore the people from whom its powers sprang, it was to be subject to annual elections. To generate support from those who might find constitutional theory too obscure, there were other more immediately appealing clauses, including demands for the end of imprisonment for debt and impressment for the army.

A Remonstrance is important for two main reasons. First, it shows Leveller recognition that a watershed in the revolution had been reached. If the conservatives in parliament had their way, the king, his powers suitably curtailed, would slip back onto his throne and there would be no more changes. In *A Remonstrance* the Levellers developed their own constitutional theory and proclaimed their challenge from the left. Second, *A Remonstrance* foreshadows the breadth of the future Leveller platform. Religious toleration remained one of their foremost demands, but it had been joined by social and economic grievances. The pamphlet was at once the statement of a radical philosophy with far-reaching constitutional implications, and the beginning of a popular programme designed to obtain maximum support.

Overton did not remain at large for long after this. In August 1646 he was arrested for a pamphlet attacking the Lords. Behaving in true Lilburnian fashion, he made sure that a crowd of Londoners witnessed his bodily removal through the streets, refused to recognise the Lords' jurisdiction and was eventually committed to Newgate. In prison he proved as adept as Lilburne in continuing his writing and the development of the Leveller campaign was not unduly hampered by the imprisonment of two of its leaders.

Lilburne took the next step. Returning to a theme he had touched on in *England's Birthright*, he devoted a whole pamphlet, *London's Liberty in Chains Discovered*, to an exposure of the oligarchical nature of the government of the City of London. Again the attack had a double purpose. In the first place it revealed how, in another sphere of government, the rights of small individuals were being trampled underfoot by a clique of moneyed men; at the same time, Lilburne was making a bid for the closer cooperation of the craftsmen of London. Thanks to the parallel between national and City politics, this stroke of expediency was wholly consistent with everything he had done so far. The liveried oligarchs of London were hand in glove with the Presbyterians in parliament and had provided substantial loans for the prosecution of the war.

Then Lilburne turned to the king. The Levellers were well aware of the continued negotiations between the Presbyterians and Charles, and the obvious way to unite opposition to any settlement that might be in the offing was to discredit the monarch. This Lilburne attempted in *Regal Tyranny Discovered*, published in January 1647, shortly before Parliament finally made terms with the Scots for the handing over of Charles to English custody. In this rather muddled pamphlet, Lilburne endeavoured to show that government should be by consent and that the institution of monarchy was incompatible with this doctrine; further, he argued, Charles was a particularly obnoxious representative of the kingly breed and should be punished with death for the treason he had committed. To support his case against the Crown, Lilburne employed the myth of the 'Norman Yoke', signs of which had already appeared in Leveller tracts. This inaccurate view of history, by no means original, told how the Norman conquest had imposed the tyranny of an alien monarchy and aristocracy upon a free, egalitarian Anglo-Saxon society in which the inhabitants had governed themselves through representative assemblies. The Levellers were not always to set so much store by this myth, realising that it was safer to ground their arguments on what *ought* to be according to God-given reason than what *had* been according to an imaginative idealisation of the past. Nevertheless, it made a useful stick with which to beat the king and the House of Lords, and became a common theme in their propaganda (**21**).

As winter slowly gave way to spring in 1647, it was apparent that events were moving towards a crisis. The Presbyterians, of whom Denzil Holles and Sir Philip Stapleton may be identified as leaders, were anxious to be rid of the army, partly because they feared its Independency and partly because its disbandment would lead to a reduction of taxation. With the king safely installed at Holdenby House, they imagined it would not be long before he accepted their terms for a return to normal conditions. The Levellers recognised the dangers. A flurry of pamphlets came from Lilburne and Overton, and there were signs of growing efficiency in the activities of their supporters in London. Professor Frank suggests that the ward-by-ward organisation in being by the end of the year had already been started, and that Walwyn, who had been strangely silent since the autumn of 1646, had probably had a hand in this development (**14**). If this is so—and the swift circulation of petitions and pamphlets supports such a view—it had no doubt been helped by discontent with rising prices consequent upon the first of the series of poor harvests. The Leveller campaign reached a climax with the publication in March of the 'Large Petition', a full-scale manifesto containing a synthesis of all Leveller thought so far [**doc. 7**].

William Walwyn was almost certainly responsible for this petition and it was characteristically moderate in tone. But it was comprehensive in content and parliament later ordered it to be burned by the common hangman—gratuitous publicity the Levellers may well have hoped for. The constitutional clauses, though they did not specifically call for the abolition of the monarchy or the House of Lords, urged the removal of their 'negative voices' and thus the end of their power. Full religious

47

toleration was demanded, together with the abolition of tithes. The main economic clauses—apart from tithes—concerned the monopolies of the Merchant Adventurers and similar companies; these were to be terminated. Turning to legal reform, the petition demanded the end of imprisonment for debt, the speeding up of judicial processes, and the translation of the law into English so that ordinary men might understand it.

Though bound to unite the landed, mercantile and legal classes in their hostility to the movement, this codification of Leveller policy was a calculated bid for mass support. Attacks on the Merchant Adventurers had a special interest for the cloth weavers. Thanks to their privileged position, the Company had a stranglehold over the industry, controlling output and prices to further their own profits. Lilburne, himself, had been prevented from setting up in the cloth trade, for which he had been trained, and had given vent to his bitterness on more than one occasion. Similarly, legal reform—particularly the end of imprisonment for debt—would evoke a response among many London craftsmen. Most of those who survived as independent masters had been forced to borrow capital and with interest rates as high as ten or twelve per cent the slide into the miseries of a debtors' prison was only too easy. The abolition of tithes had a universal appeal.

The Leveller cap was in the ring. Although the 'Large Petition' was addressed to the Commons, recent Leveller pamphlets had tended to be directed more and more towards the people themselves, over the heads of their so-called representatives. In *The Outcries of Oppressed Commons*, a joint work by Lilburne and Overton, the two prisoners had already charged the Commons with betrayal of their trust and had declared that the people were absolved from all obedience. And the people were showing interest in their self-appointed champions: a petition early in February for the release of the two men collected about 10,000 signatures. How far this civilian movement might have gone on its own is hard to say. For in March 1647, the first signs of mutiny appeared in the army and the Levellers turned their attention to military affairs. Lilburne and his friends were not likely to miss a chance like that. They had dedicated leadership and a revolutionary policy; they needed only an audience courageous enough to respond effectively. The army was destined to provide it. With the New Model on their side, the Levellers would be a force to be reckoned with.

MUTINY

Early in 1647 parliament decided to dispense with the services of the New Model Army. The last royalist garrisons had surrendered some time ago, the Scots had retired across the border, and the king was safely in residence at Holdenby, where he would no doubt soon come to see the advantages of a compromise. Only the army, victorious, confident and—at least in the view of its enemies— riddled with sectarian heresies, stood between the Presbyterians and a swift return to peacetime stability. Anxious to gain popularity by cutting taxation and to ensure that any constitutional settlement would remain wholly in its own hands, parliament voted the army's disbandment. Had parliament shown any real understanding of the men who had fought for it, the demobilisation might well have been carried through with little overt criticism. As it was, the terms of disbandment suggested at best black ingratitude, at worst outright hostility. Six weeks arrears of pay were offered to men who, as we have seen, were owned several times this amount; no security was offered for the remainder. No provision was made for those maimed in battle, or for the widows and orphans of those killed. Nor was any indemnity given to cover their actions during the war, though a number of soldiers had recently been arrested for horse-stealing and rumour had it that some had actually been hanged. The cavalry had a particular grievance: they were not to be allowed to keep their horses, although many men had originally brought their own with them and others had remounted at their own expense after the loss of horses provided by the state. Added to all this was the parliamentary proposal for a new army to subdue Ireland. This, it is true, was to consist of volunteers, but the scheme to remove Independent officers and entrust the new force to reliable conservatives did not commend itself to soldiers shrewd enough to see the motives behind it. It would be difficult to imagine a programme more likely to unite officers and men in outspoken opposition.

The first sign of disaffection was a petition circulated among the cavalry regiments in which the men demanded guarantees for arrears of pay, an indemnity, and compensation for dependents of those killed. Parliament got wind of this and summoned certain officers who were involved, including Lilburne's brother, Colonel Robert Lilburne, rebuking them for encouraging insubordination.

Analysis

Unwisely parliament went so far as to call supporters of the petition 'enemies to the state'. The next moves were more dangerous. Some time in April the troopers of the cavalry regiments began to elect representatives, known as 'agitators', to act on their behalf; at the beginning of May the foot followed suit, and by the middle of the month a council existed that could speak for the rank and file of the whole army. An open letter from the agitators followed, addressed to Fairfax, Cromwell and Skippon, in which the men appealed for the officers' support in the fight for their rights and made a provocative attack on the Presbyterians 'who have lately tasted of sovereignty . . . and seek to become masters and degenerate into tyrants'. Early in May parliament seems to have recognised some ineptitude in its handling of the disbandment. It promised a small increase in arrears—eight weeks instead of six—and an ordinance of indemnity; at the same time it dispatched four of its more sympathetic members, Skippon, Cromwell, Ireton and Fleetwood, to discuss the complaints of the men. Their meetings were with the officers rather than the ordinary soldiers, but they reported the grievances realistically on their return from the army headquarters at Saffron Walden. It remained to be seen whether the Presbyterian majority would make further concessions or force the army into open defiance.

It is hard to gauge the exact extent of Leveller influence over what Brailsford calls 'this spontaneous outbreak of democracy' in the ranks of the New Model. A good deal of evidence suggests that it was strong. Leveller pamphlets had certainly been read avidly in the army and it may have been more than mere chance that the soldiers' first petition coincided with the publication of the Levellers' 'Large Petition' in March. Edward Sexby, the most able and outspoken of the agitators had visited Lilburne in prison and distributed his pamphlets; William Allen, an Anabaptist and craftsman from London who had been imprisoned with Lilburne at Oxford, was another agitator steeped in the Leveller tradition; sympathisers among the officers included Major Tulidah and Captain John White, who had Leveller connections in London. But whatever the part played by the Levellers in the initial stages, they were soon exploiting the situation to the full. In April, just about at the time when the cavalry had been electing their first representatives, Overton published *A New Found Stratagem*, in which he openly turned to the army as 'the principal means, as things now stand, to defend and maintain your [the people's] liberties, and to keep you and yours from sudden vassalage and slavery'. Lilburne constantly received and despatched special messengers who kept him informed of the latest developments and carried his advice to the agitators. To Cromwell he sent urgent appeals to stand by the soldiers and support the opposition to disbandment. It seems likely that within a very short while army and civilian Levellers were acting as one.

The initiative behind the army petition and the election of the agitators came wholly from the ordinary soldiers of the cavalry, and throughout May they enjoyed the unaccustomed privilege of having some say in the control of their destiny. Excitement ran high. Letters, sometimes in cipher, kept them in touch with supporters in London and explained to other units of the army what was happening [**doc. 2**]. A press operated on their behalf in Oxford and a propaganda campaign was mounted in the areas where the army was quartered. Petitions were organised linking peasant grievances with those of the soldiers and showing a marked Leveller influence. But the most important problem was to gain the full cooperation of the officers. Although they were later to turn on them as reactionaries, the agitators saw that, for the time being at least, the support of the officers was vital. Several documents survive in which the officers are urged to join the men and there must have been a good deal of oral persuasion.

What was the attitude of the officers? Undoubtedly the majority was sympathetic and a few sided openly with the agitators from the beginning. But, as officers, they were suspicious of indiscipline and more aware of the problems likely to follow a blunt defiance of parliament; certainly they brought pressure to bear to moderate the tone of the soldiers' original petition. Fairfax himself was an entirely non-political figure and remained loyal to Parliament for as long as possible. When the army revolted, he wrote to both Houses explaining that he had been forced to defy them in the interests of unity and discipline. More important, and ambiguously placed because he was an M.P. as well as an officer, was Oliver Cromwell. As an Independent, he was opposed to the intolerant settlement contemplated by the Presbyterians and he was conscious of the genuine grievances of the troops; but he also saw the danger of anarchy if parliament, the last fragment of legality, should be flouted by an army mutiny. As he said during the discussions at Saffron

Walden: 'If that authority [parliament] falls to nothing, nothing can follow but confusion.' At the time, the Levellers were anxious to have him on their side and wooed his support; later, when he had become their most determined opponent, they remembered his equivocal attitude and charged him, together with his son-in-law Henry Ireton, with having 'opposed those gallant endeavours of the army for their country's freedom'. In fact, quite apart from his recognition of the complexity of the issues, Cromwell was trying to avoid taking a major political decision; as he so often did, he was waiting on the outcome of events. So he delayed, urging caution on the army and further concessions on parliament, hoping a compromise might yet obviate the need to choose between them.

It was not to be. On 25 May 1647 the Presbyterians, still bent on the destruction of the New Model and possibly lulled into a false sense of security by Cromwell's assurances that it would disband, ordered demobilisation to begin—this to be carried out regiment by regiment, each in a different place. Open revolt followed. The agitators called for a general rendezvous to guarantee unity and warned Fairfax that, with or without the officers, the men would not obey the parliamentary order. Fairfax summoned a council of war at which it was decided to oppose disbandment and to arrange a rendezvous. The officers, albeit belatedly, had thrown in their lot with the men. This made the next steps easier. Cornet Joyce seized the train of artillery at Oxford and then secured the king at Holdenby, taking him back to the army. Cromwell knew of Joyce's intention to seize the king and had probably given his consent. But the initiative throughout lay with the agitators and it seems to have been Joyce's own decision to transfer Charles to Newmarket. Fairfax was ignorant of the whole affair and the arrival of the king merely added to his perplexity. On 3 June Cromwell rode out of London and joined the army. The unfolding pattern of events, dictated by the folly of the Presbyterians and the determination of the agitators, had finally driven him to a decision.

These were heady days for the Levellers. Quite suddenly, from being a small group hovering on the fringe of the political scene, they had become a power in the land. Inspired by their own grievances but quick to grasp the relevance of Leveller doctrine, the discontented rankers fell in behind the radical banner. And already they had achievements to show. The army had not disbanded; a rendezvous had been called; the officers had taken up positions they would not have adopted of their own accord and were continuing to respond to pressures from the left.

The army assembled at Newmarket and on 5 June accepted *A Solemn Engagement of the Army*, drawn up by Ireton, in which it was declared that there would be no disbandment until grievances had been met. Furthermore, it provided for a Council of the Army in which the general officers, representatives of the other officers and the agitators were to meet to discuss policy. Even though weighted in a conservative direction, this was revolutionary indeed and must be interpreted as an attempt by the officers to make the best of a weak position. Only by inviting the agitators to join them could they hope to keep some measure of control over men threatening to destroy traditional discipline completely.

In mid-June the army confirmed its arrival in the political sphere by issuing the *Representation of the Army*, again penned by Ireton but almost certainly an amalgam of ideas put forward on the new General Council. Here for the first time it went beyond its demands for the righting of its own wrongs:

> We were not a mere mercenary army, hired to serve any arbitrary power of a state, but called forth and conjured by the several declarations of Parliament to the defence of our own and the people's just rights and liberties (**2**).

The *Representation* called for a dissolution of the existing Parliament, liberty of conscience, reform of the franchise and a redistribution of seats. Tacked on as a postscript was a charge of treason against the eleven leading Presbyterians and a demand for their expulsion from the House. It was a relatively moderate document and represented a compromise between the conservatism of the leading officers—or Grandees, as they were being called—and the extremism of the Leveller agitators. There were several signs of Leveller influence. They had been the first to demand a purge of parliament, and the clauses on the future Commons seemed to embrace the doctrine that sovereignty lies in the people and should be reflected in the composition of the House and frequent elections.

For the time being the interests of Grandees and agitators coincided. One contemporary wrote: 'It is incredible the unity of officers and soldiers.' It remained to be seen whether this alliance could be maintained.

53

Analysis

THE CASE OF THE ARMY TRULY STATED

The political situation in July 1647 was as unstable as it had been at any time since the opening of the war. The Presbyterians, frightened by the defiance of the army, made a few conciliatory gestures, but they faced a dilemma: full payment of the troops would involve the raising of a large sum of money; yet the only capital asset left to parliament was the Dean and Chapter lands and these were earmarked for the endowment of the new Presbyterian Church. The Independent Grandees found themselves taking political action none of them had anticipated. Fairfax, Cromwell, Ireton and Skippon—all had wanted the satisfaction of the soldiers' just dues followed by a peaceful disbandment. Even now they hoped the Presbyterians would make a settlement possible and were hesitant to accept the responsibilities they had inadvertently shouldered by committing themselves to the military revolt. Beneath these, the Leveller agitators were resolved not to let slip the initiative they had seized. Determined to oust Holles and his friends once for all, they urged a swift march on London. On 31 May, at the height of the crisis, Lilburne set the tone with a vicious attack on the Presbyterians in *Rash Oaths Unwarrantable,* calling on the army to destroy without mercy the 'conspiracy . . . of lawless, unlimited, and unbounded men, that have actually destroyed the laws and liberties of England'. The king no doubt smiled at the bitter divisions among his opponents. Already he savoured the thought he was later unwise enough to speak aloud: 'You cannot be without me. You will fall to ruin, if I do not sustain you.'

Whatever Charles might think, the army was the ultimate arbiter of the kingdom. And within the army tensions were growing. Strong though their own grievances were, the officers knew full well their hand had been forced by the ordinary soldiers. As the summer of 1647 drew on, the Grandees struggled to reassert their authority. Moreover, a clash between the Grandees and those who had fallen under Leveller influence was more or less certain on other than military grounds. Cromwell and his colleagues were in no sense social radicals. They belonged to the moderate gentry class that had been best represented by Pym. They had fought against the king to consolidate the gains made in 1641, not to inaugurate a social revolution. Although tending to be of lower social status than the Presbyterians, they had the same interest in maintaining stability and the sanctity of property. Only in a religious sense was Cromwell a radical; as an Independent he always supported toleration, but even here some consciences were to be regarded as more tender than others. The Levellers were more extreme in all fields and were unlikely to share common ground with the Grandees for long. The split appeared over two issues: negotiations with the king and the march on London.

With the king in their possession, the officers entered into direct negotiations for a settlement. *The Heads of the Proposals*, drawn by Ireton, represented their offer and gives the clearest view of the fundamentally conservative agreement the Grandees wanted. A brief summary must suffice here. It was intended to restore the king, who was to be assisted by biennial parliaments and a Council of State, the composition of which was to be controlled largely by parliament. Deferring to Charles's intense religious beliefs, the existence of the episcopacy was allowed for, but there was to be full toleration, at least for Protestants. These were generous terms which show the Independents' desire to restore the system they knew, with suitable checks on the Crown. The rôle of the Levellers in drawing up this offer is obscure. Twelve agitators sat on the committee that considered it, but Wildman charged Ireton with arbitrary behaviour and it is possible that it was never laid before the full Council of the Army. Certainly it is difficult to believe that the Levellers, who had long ago rejected king and lords, should support wholeheartedly such a backward-looking document. Nevertheless, there were signs that Ireton was trying to placate opinion on the left. *The Heads of the Proposals* spoke of legal reform, including a change in the law of imprisonment for debt, abolition of monopolies, and even suggested —Ireton walking a tightrope here—that the vexed question of tithes should be reconsidered. Such concessions reveal Ireton's recognition of Leveller strength, but were unlikely wholly to dissipate the growing suspicion that the Grandees had little sympathy for Leveller ideas and were going to do a deal with the king at the first opportunity. When the king rejected these terms at the end of July, before the capture of London, he was not only rejecting the most generous offer he was likely to receive, he was also driving the moderates into the arms of the extremists.

Meanwhile the Grandees and agitators had also fallen out over the attitude to be adopted towards the Presbyterians in Parliament. The former still hoped agreement could be reached and were

anxious to avoid open force. In an attempt to bring the Presbyterians to their senses they manoeuvred the army threateningly
around London. The agitators pressed for action. In a debate of the
General Council of the Army held at Reading, they argued for a
swift march on the capital to pull the Presbyterians out by the ears
Having started the revolt in the first place, they had fewer qualms
about the use of the sword. Moreover, they were acutely conscious
of the continued imprisonment of Lilburne and Overton; indeed
even while the discussions at Reading were taking place, Overton
published a stirring call to the army—'now the only formal and
visible head that is left unto the people'—to remove the tyrannical
Presbyterians and right the wrongs of people like himself. The
exchanges at Reading were brisk, and notable for the way in which
Levellers like Allen and Sexby stood up to their superior officers
Eventually a compromise was reached: the army delayed its march
but sent an ultimatum to Parliament demanding, among other
points, the immediate removal of the eleven leading Presbyterians
from the House. A postscript called for the speedy trial or release or
bail of Lilburne, Overton and other Levellers. This was a setback
for the agitators. Cromwell and Ireton had not been stampeded into
direct action and the postscript was a much watered-down version
of the agitators' original demand. Nevertheless, events continued to
move in the Levellers' favour and the Grandees were soon forced
to take a tougher line.

Initially the ultimatum had the desired effect. Holles and the
other named Presbyterians retired from the House, and the City
militia was taken out of Presbyterian hands; nothing was done for the
imprisoned Levellers, but Parliament was right in believing that, for
the Grandees at least, Lilburne and Overton did not constitute a
high priority. However, other pressures were at work in the City
Backed by the governing oligarchy, a City mob sought to stiffen the
resolution of the wavering Presbyterian M.P.s Invading both Houses
the rioters enforced the passage of motions reversing the decision on
control of the militia and inviting the king to London. Both Speakers
eight peers and fifty-seven Independent M.P.s promptly fled from
London to the army. In their absence the eleven Presbyterians return
ed, a Committee of Safety was set up, and the City gathered its troop
together to face the New Model, whose attack was now inevitable.

The happenings in London drove the Grandees towards the
Leveller position; the New Model could delay no longer. The excuse

of returning Speakers, peers and M.P.s to their rightful place gave Cromwell and Ireton the cloak of legality they desired. So the army marched. At first it seemed likely that the City would resist, but its courage failed as Fairfax advanced and the capital was taken without bloodshed. The Levellers played a significant part in the operation. Colonel Rainsborough, the Leveller soon to be prominent in the Putney debates, led an encircling movement to the south of the Thames and was admitted to Southwark by sympathisers within. Southwark had long resented the riches and power on the other side of the river and was always a fruitful source of Leveller support.

The capture of London solved nothing; the situation remained as fluid as before. The eleven Presbyterians had fled, but their cause still enjoyed a majority in the House and there was a growing demand in the army for a full-scale purge. The king continued to negotiate at all points of the compass. He openly said he preferred the army proposals to those of Parliament, but was determined to improve them; in the meanwhile he intrigued with the Scots for a re-opening of the war. Despite the king's deceit, well known to the Grandees by mid-October, Cromwell and Ireton remained dedicated to the restoration of the monarchy; the ideal of a balanced 'Elizabethan' constitution dominated their thinking and seemed the only guarantee of a return to stability. In the Commons a small republican group, headed by Henry Marten—himself no stranger to the Levellers—was roundly defeated when it proposed a vote of 'no further addresses' to the king. But with power firmly in the hands of the army, the most important development in the autumn of 1647 was the growing estrangement between Grandees and agitators.

The Levellers never really trusted the Grandees. Both Lilburne and Overton urged the men to beware of their officers. 'Trust your great officers', advised Lilburne in August, 'no farther than you can throw an ox.' Their behaviour after the seizure of London confirmed these suspicions. Parliament was not purged; negotiations with the king dragged on inconclusively; and, most important from the Leveller point of view, Lilburne and Overton remained in prison. Cromwell paid Lilburne a friendly visit in the Tower, but made it plain that he would not be released unless he would promise not 'to make new hurley-burlies' in the army. Caught between the crossfire of Presbyterians on the right and Levellers on the left, the Grandees did not intend to add to their embarrassments by allowing

Lilburne a free hand with the agitators. These disappointments led to a new burst of Leveller energy aimed at regaining the initiative lost when the men's representatives had been absorbed into the General Council. Rumours spread that Cromwell had been bribed by Charles with the promise of the earldom of Essex and the garter— a story with a Presbyterian origin but which suited the Leveller book equally well. In a public letter to Henry Marten, Lilburne announced that since Cromwell had failed him and planned 'to keep the poor people everlastingly . . . in bondage and slavery', he would henceforth appeal to the ordinary soldiers. Probably at Lilburne's instigation, several regiments elected new, and more extreme, agitators. Finally, in October, the agitators of five regiments stationed in Surrey signed *The Case of the Army Truly Stated*, a manifesto drawn up by civilian and army Levellers, among whom the guiding hand of John Wildman may be distinguished [**doc. 3**].

Amidst its discursive and repetitive argument, *The Case of the Army* had one main aim: to unite the soldiers and ordinary people. Its authors were conscious of the growing unpopularity of the army as time passed, heavy taxation continued, and disbandment seemed as far away as ever. *The Case of the Army* constituted a stirring indictment of the army leadership and a call to the soldiers and civilians to rally behind the Levellers. There were stern criticisms of 'the present manner of actings of many at the Headquarters' and the 'supine negligence' of 'many whom we did betrust'. Five months of frustration had led to complete disillusionment. The Grandees seemed more concerned with putting the king back on his throne than dealing with the grievances in the army and country at large. The solution, it was argued, lay in adherence to a common cause—the full Leveller programme.

The social and economic clauses of *The Case of the Army* embodied the usual Leveller demands—religious toleration, legal reform, abolition of tithes, excise and monopolies—but in their agitation for army pay the authors showed a new sensitivity to the feelings of the civilian population. Arrears should not, they suggested, be raised by taxation, but by the sale of Dean and Chapter lands; and strict accounts should be kept to prevent repetition of the corruption that had already taken place. But the constitutional proposals were the most striking. Under these there would be biennial Parliaments, to be elected by all free-born men of twenty-one and over who were not delinquents (royalists), and, to ensure the continuation of this scheme, the Levellers postulated a 'law paramount' as distinct from ordinary legislation dealt with by Parliament. The implications of the franchise proposal will be considered later, but a word more is necessary here on the 'law paramount'.

The Case of the Army was based on the already familiar premise that 'all power is originally and essentially in the whole body of the people'. But successive bodies had failed in their trust: the king, parliament, and recently the army. Even if Leveller constitutional plans came to fruition, there would be every chance that some future parliament might change the system and reconstruct it according to its own corrupt lights. The Levellers sought a guarantee for the sovereignty of the people, a guarantee for certain basic rights shortly to be enumerated in the *Agreement of the People* [**doc. 5**]. This they found in the 'law paramount'—a law based on right reason, and quite unalterable once recognised. Thus far had the Levellers come since their first pleas for religious toleration and Lilburne's legalistic quibbles before Commons and Lords.

THE FIRST DEFEAT: PUTNEY AND WARE

The Case of the Army was presented to Fairfax in the middle of October 1647 and it was agreed that the Leveller proposals should be considered by the General Council of the Army. But *The Case* was an unwieldy document and its wording was bound to antagonise the senior officers; so before the Council met the Levellers extracted the main constitutional proposals and incorporated them in a concise, straightforward paper—*An Agreement of the People for a firm Peace*. It is not known who was its draughtsman, but it may well have been a collective effort involving Lilburne, Walwyn, Overton and Wildman.

The Levellers' justification for an entirely new constitution was simple and already familiar to readers of their pamphlets. The old state had collapsed, they claimed; the Civil War and subsequent events had returned the country to a state of nature in which anarchy prevailed and every man had to fight for survival as best he could; only a new constitution supported by the whole population could re-found civil society and government. Thinking in terms of the religious covenants in which members of Independent congregations subscribed to certain beliefs and disciplines, the Levellers

Analysis

put forward the *Agreement* as a social contract to be the basis of a new community. Whether conceived in secular or religious terms, the idea of a contract was part of the mental furniture of seventeenth-century political thinkers and it was natural for the Levellers to base their Utopia upon it. Moreover, the existence of the New Model Army did something to solve the problem facing any contract theorist of how to obtain the consent of *everybody*. The army was a fair cross section of English society and might be used, at least to begin with, as a basis for the contract; it would then only remain to associate the civilians with the *Agreement*—an association already foreshadowed by the open bid for civilian cooperation in *The Case of the Army*.

The *Agreement of the People* was brief and to the point. It demanded the dissolution of the Long Parliament and biennial parliaments in future. Seats would be redistributed to coincide more nearly with the distribution of population and Parliament would have full executive authority. This power, 'inferior only to theirs who choose them', would be limited by certain inalienable individual rights: religious toleration, freedom from impressment, and equality before the law [**doc. 5**]. Though not stated in so many words, these last were guaranteed by the 'law paramount'. Plainly there was no room for the king or lords in such a scheme and they were ignored completely. The very important suffrage provision in *The Case of the Army* was a strange omission, but as the debate on the *Agreement* developed it became clear that it was implied in the clause dealing with equal electoral districts. The *Agreement* was, in fact, only a sketch of the Levellers' full programme and later versions of it were much more comprehensive, including those economic demands which had the greatest appeal for the mass of the population.

The General Council met in the church at Putney in the closing days of October and it was not long before the discussions revealed the basic differences between the Grandees, the new conservatives of the revolution, and their fiery critics on the left. The main protagonists were, for the Grandees, Ireton and Cromwell, and for the Levellers, Rainsborough, Sexby, Allen, and two co-opted civilians, Wildman and one Maximilian Petty. To ensure that they were not misrepresented, the Levellers circulated appeals to the soldiers to stand by their representatives and not to trust such proven deceivers as Cromwell and Ireton. They anticipated a troubled passage for the *Agreement* and Sexby's opening speech, again highly critical of the Grandees, suggests that the Levellers recognised that they no longer held the initiative as they had in the hectic days of May.

The first exchanges centred on the desirability of considering the Leveller constitution at all. Cromwell was obstructive from the start and, after pointing out 'the very great mountains in the way' of such revolutionary proposals, contended that the *Agreement* would break the engagements to which the army was committed in its various declarations. This led down a blind alley of ethical controversy about the need to keep engagements which might be unjust—a controversy only ended when Colonel Goffe, an Anabaptist, called on the Council to hold a prayer meeting to seek the will of God. That this suggestion was followed is impressive witness to the strong religious overtones of the debates; that it resolved nothing underlines the fundamental nature of the division between the two sides.

After these preliminary skirmishings, the main battle was joined over the question of the suffrage. When the *Agreement* was eventually read, Ireton asked bluntly whether the redistribution of seats according to the number of inhabitants meant that every man was to have the vote. To this Petty replied: 'We judge that all inhabitants that have not lost their birthright should have an equal voice in elections.' More passionately, Rainsborough, whose outbursts so frequently accounted for the acrimony of the debates, said:

> For really I think that the poorest he that is in England hath a life to live, as the greatest he; and therefore truly, sir, I think it's clear, that every man that is to live under a government ought first by his own consent to put himself under that government . . . (**2**).

Whatever the exact meaning of the Leveller suffrage proposals, these are democratic sentiments and remarkable for their day and age.

Ireton was shocked and his riposte outlined the justification for the property qualifications that were to remain the basis of English political life until the Reform Bills of the nineteenth century:

> No person hath a right to an interest or share in the disposing of the affairs of the kingdom, and in determining or choosing those that shall determine what laws we shall be ruled by here—no person hath a right to this that hath not a permanent fixed interest in this kingdom . . . (**2**).

Analysis

For Ireton, 'a permanent fixed interest' meant ownership of free-hold land or membership as a freeman of a trading corporation. Only such persons were likely to adopt a responsible attitude to the problems of government.

Here for a brief moment in the little church at Putney, the English Revolution was poised on the knife-edge between reform and reaction. The debate swayed to and fro, sometimes moderate, more frequently impassioned, always tense. Rainsborough justified an extension of the franchise by appealing to God-given reason and the law of nature. Ireton countered by claiming that any resort to a law of nature by which everyone is free and equal would mean the destruction of all property rights and the consequent dissolution of civil society. Finding themselves being pushed into a false position, the Levellers, who were neither anarchists nor communists—after all, their most important supporters were small property owners—hotly denied the charge that they favoured anarchy. Nevertheless, they thought it odd that the vote had come into the private owner-ship of some men and not others, and were quick to point out the unjust anomaly that most of the ordinary soldiers who had won the war were likely to find themselves without any say in the governing of the country [**doc. 6**]. Furthermore, while not prepared to deny property rights, Sexby and others hinted strongly that individual rights are more important and suggested that emphasis on property qualification was merely an excuse for the few rich to oppress the many poor. Ireton, cool and assured, expressed the traditional view with logic and clarity. As so often in these crucial years, he seemed possessed of the most impressive intellect of any of the Grandees; certainly Cromwell was prepared to leave matters largely in his able son-in-law's hands. The Levellers—a term first used at Putney—while feeling their way tentatively towards the democracy implicit in their belief in the sovereignty of the people, were increasingly handicapped by insinuations that they were greater social revolutionaries than they really were.

What exactly were the Levellers' franchise proposals? From the relevant clause in *The Case of the Army* and extravagant statements like that of Rainsborough quoted above, it would seem that they favoured manhood suffrage. In fact, this was not so. As the debate progressed, it became apparent that two important groups were to be excluded—servants and those in receipt of alms. Such persons, it was explained by Petty, 'depended upon the will of other men and should be afraid to displease them', and servants were 'included in their masters'. This much is clear. Historians disagree, however, when they try to decide exactly what constituted a 'servant'. Taking the view that the Levellers intended to deny the franchise to all who had lost their economic independence—or 'lost their birthright', as they put it—Professor C. B. Macpherson believes the term 'servant' to have been a loose definition covering all in receipt of wages, a thesis apparently supported by the second *Agreement of the People*, drawn up a year later, which explicitly excludes wage-earners (**23**). Mr Peter Laslett holds that the word 'servant' needs to be more narrowly defined (**31**). Seventeenth-century society, he argues, was essentially patriarchal and the crucial unit in the structure of society was the household. A 'servant' was a person who *lived in* his master's house and the term would not normally have applied to wage-earners who were heads of their own households. Under this definition, living-out wage-earners might have been included in the Leveller franchise at Putney and their later exclusion could be interpreted as a move towards compromise with the Independents. Whichever view is correct, a substantial number of people would not have gained the vote. There were strict limitations on the Leveller brand of democracy.

Nevertheless, the gap between Independent Grandees and Levellers remained wide. The Grandees held out for a freehold property qualification; the Leveller scheme would have enfranchised the craftsmen and shopkeepers in the towns as well as the bulk of the copyhold and leasehold farmers. A committee was set up in an attempt to reconcile the *Agreement* with the officers' ideas as expressed in the *Heads of the Proposals*. On this committee the Grandees had the upper hand and the compromise reached made only a few concessions to the Levellers. All who had fought for parliament were to be given the vote and there was to be a redistribution of seats; but the question of any further extension of the franchise was evaded and it was assumed that king and lords would be restored. When these proposals were read to the full Council by Ireton, Wildman, who had not been on the committee, made numerous interruptions and asked what powers of veto over Commons' legislation were to be given to crown and peers. Here the Grandees were in a dilemma: as conservatives anxious to restore the traditional structure of government and as politicians who needed to conciliate royalist and Presbyterian opinion, they favoured the privileges of the king and the Upper House; but as men who had been forced by circumstances to adopt revolutionary postures throughout 1647 and who had gone a long way towards acceptance of the Leveller creed of the sovereignty of the people, they found such privileges hard to justify. In the event, Ireton argued that while the Commons would be the supreme legislator for the ordinary people, their laws would not be binding on the king and peers themselves unless they gave their consent—a plainly unsatisfactory solution unlikely to please anybody.

But these fascinating debates were nearing their end. Ever since the beginning of June when he had thrown in his lot with the agitators, Cromwell had realised that the army was the only guarantee for peace in the kingdom and that it only remained such a guarantee while under its officers' control. As the discussions at Putney progressed, he saw this discipline endangered by the extremists in the General Council. The Levellers outvoted the Grandees for the restoration of their full suffrage proposals to the emasculated draft; a Leveller motion was carried for another general rendezvous; and a letter was sent to the Commons asking that no further addresses be made to the king—a direct criticism of the Grandees, who favoured continued negotiations. The signs were ominous and Cromwell launched an immediate counter-attack. He had a resolution passed that officers and agitators should return to their regiments pending the rendezvous; having scattered the troublemakers, he ensured that they should not re-unite by arranging the rendezvous in three separate places; lastly, he 'packed' another committee, whose task was to draft a non-controversial document for presentation to the troops.

While striving to prevent Leveller domination of the General Council, Cromwell found an unexpected ally. On 11 November the king fled from Hampton Court to the Isle of Wight. Several contemporaries charged Cromwell with complicity in the escape, for with the resurrection of the royalist threat he now had ample excuse to enforce strict discipline. In fact, he almost certainly had nothing to do with it. Charles, pleading that the Levellers were planning to murder him, simply wanted greater freedom for his negotiations with the Scots—negotiations already close to the treaty that produced the second Civil War. There is no evidence that the Levellers had any assassination plans at this time, though, as several speakers made clear at Putney, they were keen to bring the 'man of blood' to trial. Whatever the truth of the matter, Cromwell's hand was strengthened for the critical meetings shortly to take place.

Leveller hopes of recreating the exhilaration of the early days at Newmarket were sadly disappointed by the new rendezvous. Of the three rendezvous appointed, only the one at Corkbush Field, Ware, produced trouble for the Grandees. There two regiments, Harrison's and Robert Lilburne's, turned up against orders and with copies of the *Agreement* stuck in their hats. Harrison's cavalry removed the offending documents after an address from Fairfax, but Lilburne's foot refused and the officers had to go in amongst them to pull them out. Cromwell is often credited with riding into the mutinous ranks with drawn sword but evidence for this is slight (**13**). Several ringleaders were arrested and three were condemned to death immediately by drumhead court martial. These diced for their lives and the loser, one Arnold, was shot in front of his regiment.

The Ware rendezvous was a notable victory for the Grandees. The seven regiments officially summoned accepted the moderate policy statement without fuss; the two mutinous regiments had wavered in the face of determined action and discipline had been restored with a minimum of bloodshed. For the Levellers it was a sharp setback. Although John Lilburne, recently released on bail, had hastened to Ware, Leveller plans had been uncoordinated. With their army supporters divided at three points, unity of action was difficult enough; but there was not even unity of intent. The agitators had circulated a critical account of the Grandees' handling of the Putney debates and Rainsborough tried to present a copy of the *Agreement* to Fairfax on his arrival at the rendezvous, but Sexby, who was present, seems to have taken no action at all.

Undoubtedly the flight of the king had much to do with this indecision; the possibility of renewed civil war must have made any attack on the officers seem inopportune. Moreover, there was some suspicion among the agitators that the royalists were trying to foment discontent in the army on their own account and this too would have acted as a brake on their enthusiasm. Nevertheless, whatever excuses may be made, Corkbush Field was a major reverse. Having helped to dictate the pace and direction of events for the last six months, the Levellers found at this vital point that the New Model remained a disciplined body with a powerful loyalty to Fairfax and Cromwell. It must have seemed to the London Levellers, who had been in constant touch with the agitators and who had pinned such high hopes on the army, that the counter-revolution had begun.

In a sense it had. Cromwell and his fellow Grandees never again moved as rapidly to the left as they did during the summer of 1647 when they had so frequently been forced to keep step with the agitators. They were stronger as a result of the showdown at Ware and a meeting of the General Council at Windsor on 8 January 1648 was probably the last to which the representatives of the men were invited; all subsequent attempts to revive the agitator movement were promptly suppressed. And the Grandees could afford to be merciful. Several men involved in the mutiny had to run the gauntlet, but later all prisoners were released and all sentences quashed.

For the time being the military wing of the movement had failed. But the Levellers were far from moribund and their continued influence in the army could not be ignored. Paradoxically, even as Cromwell crushed the incipient mutiny he was himself abandoning one of the key positions he had defended at Putney. By the end of 1647 he was beginning to have grave doubts about the possibility of any settlement with the king.

'COZENED AND DECEIVED'

The Grandees had good reason to be disappointed with the man whose rights they had defended throughout 1647. Not only had he rejected the *Heads of the Proposals* in characteristically arrogant fashion and broken his parole by fleeing to the Isle of Wight, but he was also cheerfully dragging the country to the brink of renewed civil war by his dealings with the Scots. Exasperation with the king was stimulated by other factors: the bleak economic situation following another poor harvest and a particularly severe winter; disturbing symptoms of royalism in several parts of the country, not least in the City itself; and, above all, the attitude of the still unpaid army. In spite of their success at Ware, the Grandees saw how brittle was army discipline after the excitements of 1647; they knew the growing strength of feeling against the king among the ordinary soldiers and their own vulnerability to Leveller propaganda while they continued to treat with him. 'If we cannot bring the army to our sense, we must go to theirs', remarked Cromwell. After Charles had turned down a new parliamentary offer on 28 December (the Four Bills), the reversal of the Grandees' position came into the open and Cromwell supported a successful motion of 'no addresses' in the Commons. Once again Cromwell had moved towards the Levellers. The king was a pace nearer the scaffold.

This conversion of the Grandees gave some unanimity to the final sessions of the General Council at Windsor. It did not satisfy the civilian Levellers, who were more conscious of the treatment of their supporters at Ware than the Grandees' sudden recognition of the king's duplicity. Lilburne claimed that the courts martial under which the mutineers had been punished were illegal in *England's Freedom, Soldiers' Rights*, and Wildman flayed his recent debating opponents in *Putney Projects*, a scornful denunciation of Cromwell, Ireton and the monarchical principle they had defended. The violence of this assault reflected not so much disillusionment—the Levellers never had many illusions about the officers—as fury at Leveller impotence in the recent trial of strength and dismay that the *Agreement* had been shelved. They now made the *Agreement* the centre of their activity in London. Two petitions exhorting the Commons to consider it were circulated and presented to the House. The Commons, who had already congratulated Cromwell officially for putting down the mutiny, showed even less sympathy than the Grandees and five more Levellers were imprisoned. This brusque treatment by both army commanders and parliament convinced the Levellers that they had to rely entirely on their own resources. The aim now was to perfect the party organisation so that public opinion could be mobilised effectively and brought into play in the existing political vacuum.

The need to circulate petitions had resulted in an embryonic party organisation at an early stage. By 1648 this had reached a high degree of efficiency. At the lowest level, each ward of the City had a cell of supporters and organisers; at the top, a committee of twelve elected agents directed policy. The expenses of printing and distributing pamphlets were defrayed from subscriptions ranging from twopence to half a crown a week according to means; Thomas Prince and Samuel Chidley were the elected treasurers. The headquarters of the party were at the Whalebone Tavern, where the executive committee met thrice weekly, and each ward had its own tavern for sympathisers. The Levellers were less successful in extending their influence beyond London, but Buckinghamshire, Hertfordshire and Kent seem to have had well organised groups who kept in touch with events in the City. The party had its own newspaper, *The Moderate*, originally a drab Puritan news-sheet with a dwindling circulation. Some time in the summer of 1648 it fell under Leveller control, becoming lively, controversial, and to judge from its increased size, economically viable. With correspondents reporting from provincial centres as far apart as Chester, Bristol and Newcastle, *The Moderate* did something to give the party a national flavour.

One of the most notable characteristics of the Levellers was their resilience in adversity, and once they had worked the recriminations for Putney out of their system they devoted themselves to a fresh propaganda campaign. Again a petition was its focal point. Difficult to suppress without popular odium, and informative to those who read and signed them, the mass petition was a formidable weapon and an essential feature of Leveller strategy. The *Earnest Petition* of January 1648 had an importance of its own. There are two interesting additions to the Leveller programme. First, the belief in the sovereignty of the people now led to the demand that all magistrates should be elected by the inhabitants of the area in which they were to serve. This would have meant not only decentralisation, but also the weakening of the landed classes whose social and economic superiority was enhanced by their position as J.P.s. Secondly, the petition called for the abolition of the excise tax—which bore more heavily on the poor than the rich—and the substitution of direct taxation 'according to the proportion of men's estates'. Significant though these clauses are, the most illuminating aspect of this document is the growing political maturity of the Levellers. Hitherto, guided by enthusiastic idealism, they had exhibited more valour than sense as they struck out in all directions. Now they were aware of the needs of expediency. If the Grandees were their enemies, it was necessary to make conciliatory gestures towards the Presbyterians. Tithe abolition was omitted from this petition and religious toleration, the original ground of dispute with the Presbyterians, only gained a brief mention. Moreover, the Levellers appreciated the advantages that might accrue from the prevailing conditions. Lilburne—for he wrote the petition—talked of 'thousands of families impoverished' and the 'merciless famine . . . entered into our gates'. Among his proposals for alleviating distress was one to raise the wages of the poorer labourers. It is not necessary to doubt

Lilburne's sincerity to argue that he was wittingly laying more emphasis on economic demands with a broad appeal than on the abstruse points of political theory debated at Putney.

Lilburne's activities as a party organiser were soon brought to the attention of the Commons by an informer who attended a party meeting at Wapping. His bail was withdrawn and, with the usual scenes of popular excitement, he was returned to the Tower. Wildman was also imprisoned, in the Fleet. Both were still in gaol when the long-threatened second Civil War broke out in the spring of 1648.

The second war was an untidy affair. After protracted negotiations, Charles had reached agreement with the Scots in December 1647 and both parties signed the Engagement, by which the king accepted the Presbyterian Church for three years. But it was general discontent in England, stemming in the main from economic hardships, that led to renewed fighting on Charles's behalf. Revolt flared in south Wales and was shortly followed by outbursts in the north, in Kent, and in Essex; nearly half the navy mutinied and joined the royalists. In July a Scottish force under Hamilton crossed the border. For a while it seemed possible that the assorted forces mustered under the king's banner might be successful. But they lacked unity. Months of intrigue had sapped their trust in each other and the man for whom they fought. Hard-core royalists found it difficult to welcome their new Presbyterian allies. The English Presbyterians were split among themselves and though willing to talk to the king were not anxious to fight for him; in any case they were highly suspicious of the Scots. The Scots, too, were divided and the Engagement was denounced by many who refused to support an uncovenanted king; as a result, Leslie's seasoned troops were unavailable for the invasion and Hamilton's force contained many raw levies. The New Model acted swiftly and decisively: the internal revolts were suppressed; the Scots were cut to pieces at Preston. By the end of August, the king's cause had failed again.

What was the attitude of the Levellers throughout the summer of 1648? Lilburne's first pamphlets after his return to the Tower castigated Cromwell and Ireton as 'usurping tyrants, and destroyers of law and liberty', but when fighting was renewed he remained quiet. Whatever their feelings about the Independent Grandees, the Levellers saw that the Royalist–Presbyterian coalition had to be destroyed before they could press their own case. Lilburne himself made this clear. On 1 August, after the presentation of a petition for his freedom signed by more than 10,000, the Commons voted his release and the payment of the reparations due for his treatment by Star Chamber; on the day following, the Lords annulled their sentence on him. Undoubtedly the main motive behind this sudden burst of generosity was the hope of the Presbyterian interest, still commanding a majority in Parliament, that Lilburne would create trouble for the Grandees in general and Cromwell in particular. In the event, Lilburne wrote immediately to Cromwell, pledging his support for the current campaign and boasting, in his inimitable way, that he scorned to strike a man while he was low—'if ever my hand be upon you, it shall be when you are in full glory'.

Recognition that this was hardly the time to rock the boat was not the only Leveller consideration. The political scene was changing and once again events were putting the Levellers in a favourable strategic position: circumstances continued to force the Grandees nearer to the Leveller view of the king. The mood of the officers' meeting held at Windsor as the fighting started augured ill for Charles. The officers reproached themselves for their advances to him and several strongly hinted that he should be brought to trial. Moreover, the Grandees, though firmly in command of the army, found themselves increasingly isolated. They had thrown over the king, yet had disturbing evidence of his popularity in the country at large. The Presbyterians had moved further off than ever. Taking advantage of the army's absence, the Presbyterian leaders had returned; more steps were taken towards the intolerance of a full Presbyterian system; the vote of 'no addresses' passed under army pressure was repealed and by the end of September new negotiations had started with Charles at Newport in the Isle of Wight. Nor was this all. The Grandees' allies in parliament, the civilian Independents, had shown some inclination to support new overtures to the king. Sir Henry Vane was actually appointed one of the parliamentary commissioners to treat with him. The Grandees felt weak; they had little choice but to turn to the Levellers.

The Levellers were sensitive to the new situation developing. In September they drew up yet another petition, a document notable for its emphasis on themes to which the Independents might be expected to be sympathetic and its omission of demands likely to lead to friction. All signs of concessions to the Presbyterians vanished.

70

The petition concentrated on the misdoings of parliament, in particular its proposal to renew contact with the king, and called for a dissolution; it also urged the trial and punishment of Charles. The constitutional plans were, by Leveller standards, moderate. The individual rights enumerated in the *Agreement* were included, the demand for religious toleration being particularly blunt and vigorous; but the future existence of monarchy and Lords was implicitly recognised, though they were to be deprived of their 'negative voices'. There was no mention of extending the franchise and a significant clause condemned any attempt to abolish property rights; the Levellers were determined to avoid the misrepresentation they had suffered at Putney.

The September Petition had a double purpose: it not only suggested the Levellers' willingness to form a radical alliance with the Grandees to thwart any treaty produced by the king and parliament, but it was also designed as a show of strength. The Levellers claimed 40,000 signatures and the *Moderate* reported petitions of support from, among others, Cornish tin-miners, Somerset cloth-weavers and various regiments of the army. The Petition was rejected by parliament, but it helped to convince the Grandees of the value of Leveller assistance.

The second Civil War was not all gain for the Levellers. One of the royalist strongholds to survive the general collapse of the summer was Pontefract and here siege operations continued. Among the siege experts sent north to help was Rainsborough. At the end of October, two royalists invaded Rainsborough's lodgings in Doncaster and tried to carry him off, intending to hold him until he could be exchanged for the royalist prisoner, Sir Marmaduke Langdale. Impulsive to the last, Rainsborough, though unarmed, set on his kidnappers and fought until he was killed. The loss of a man of his calibre and in his influential position just as Levellers and army leaders were coming together again was a considerable misfortune. With genuine emotion and, it must be admitted, their usual flair for publicity, the Levellers arranged an impressive funeral in London, the large crowds of mourners wearing sea-green ribbons, Rainsborough's colour, which became thereafter the colour of the party.

The September Petition and Rainsborough's funeral gave a fair indication of the revival of Leveller fortunes. The initiative, however, lay with the Grandees and at this critical stage they were unable to present a united front. Fairfax, undeterred by the embittered feelings of his men, still favoured a settlement with the king. Cromwell could not make up his mind. His ability to take decisive action, so sure in battle, frequently deserted him in the political field. His absence from London in the autumn of 1648—he was at Pontefract —provides a classic example of his waiting until his hand was forced. In the same way had he waited in May 1647 until there had been no choice but to follow the lead of the agitators. Only one man was prepared to take a positive line: Henry Ireton. On 10 November Ireton presented to the Council of the army the draft of his *Remonstrance*, in which he called for the punishment of the king. Whether impressed by the ordinary soldiers, whose petitions asked for justice on those responsible for the war, or convinced by his own cold logic of the necessity for Charles's death as the prerequisite of any lasting settlement, Ireton pressed consistently for the king's trial in the confusion of the weeks that followed.

Yet it was Cromwell, undecided about the king's fate but conscious of the Grandees' isolation, who first put out feelers to the Levellers. He kept in touch with Lilburne after his release and suggested that certain Levellers and Independents should meet to discuss a possible constitution settlement. The conferences between the two sides took place early in November and provide an admirable opportunity for the analysis of their relative positions. The extreme Independents—for those attending represented the body of opinion following Ireton—were concerned with the immediate political situation. Following the pragmatic tradition developed by the Independents over the two previous years, they wanted the execution of the king and the purge or dissolution of parliament to come first; once Charles and the Presbyterians were out of the way, the Grandees could solve the constitutional problem. The Levellers did not share this view. Lilburne and Wildman, who put their case, were more interested in the final constitutional solution and shrewdly judged that if king and parliament were removed there would be no check at all on the swords of the Grandees. Paradoxically, Lilburne, who had been the first to demand the king's death, now argued for his preservation until safeguards against military dictatorship could be drawn up (**13, 14**).

Eventually, a new and shortlived idea was put forward: that there should be a national convention, comprising military and civilian members, which would thrash out a constitution. In the meanwhile, the representatives urged a revision of Ireton's *Remonstrance* with the inclusion of the main points of the Levellers' September Petition. The *Remonstrance of the Army* presented to parliament on 20 November showed unmistakable signs of a shift towards the Levellers. The idea of a national convention was ignored, but it demanded biennial parliaments unhampered by the negative voices of king or lords, and the establishment of the constitution 'by a general contract or agreement of the people'. The franchise was not mentioned, but these amendments indicate Ireton's apparent acceptance of the Leveller creed of the sovereignty of the people.

Whether spurred on by these concessions or suspicious that the Grandees were merely buying Leveller silence while they hustled the king into oblivion, Lilburne and Wildman rode to Windsor to meet Ireton face to face. A stormy scene took place at the Garter Inn; no agreement was reached and the Levellers retired, threatening to inflame public opinion in London. Here was a crisis for the Independents and one that took the Levellers to a glimpse of real power. There were rumours of an impending treaty at Newport. If king and parliament should unite and order the disbandment of the army, a second mutinous refusal would be impossible to justify; certainly Fairfax would support the tattered remnants of the old régime. Committed as he was to the removal of the king, Ireton had to neutralise his enemies on the left while he dealt with those on the right. So Colonel Harrison, his staunchest supporter, hastened after Lilburne's party and caught them at their lodgings on the point of departure. There, shortly before midnight, a compromise was reached which temporarily allied Levellers and Independents. At the Levellers' suggestion, a committee was to be set up consisting of four representatives of the army, four parliamentary Independents, four City Independents, and four Levellers. These representatives were charged to draw up a new Agreement of the People, to come into effect once king and Long Parliament had been destroyed. For a brief moment it seemed that the Levellers had achieved part of their dream: the mobilisation of the whole army behind their constitutional theory.

Strengthened by this alliance, the Grandees acted. On 1 December the king was seized and transferred to Hurst Castle; on 2 December Fairfax and the army entered London; on 6 December Colonel Pride began his purge of the Commons, leaving behind a 'rump' of Independents. Cromwell, carefully absent while these decisions were being taken, arrived from the north the next day. He still had his doubts over the necessity for the king's death, but Charles's continued intransigence soon converted him to Ireton's view.

Meanwhile the four Leveller members of the committee—Lilburne, Walwyn, Wildman and Petty—drafted a new Agreement and put it forward for the consideration of their colleagues on the full committee—on which there were only thirteen members, three of the parliamentary Independents having failed to appear. At length, a majority accepted an amended version of the Leveller document. It was at this point, so Lilburne later claimed, that the Levellers realised they had been 'cozened and deceived' by the 'cunningest of Machiavellians . . . Ireton'. Lilburne always professed to believe that his agreement with Harrison at Windsor, endorsed verbally by Ireton, had given the members of the negotiating committee plenipotentiary powers; that the new constitution, once ratified by the representatives, would automatically be accepted as the law of the land without further alteration by anybody. In fact, it was passed to the Council of Officers who promptly started to dismember it. Whatever the truth of the matter, it was extremely naïve of Lilburne to imagine the army would adopt the Agreement without discussion, though it was perhaps in keeping with his constant overestimation of his party's importance. He did not understand that the alliance with the Grandees was built on their temporary weakness rather than the Levellers' strength. Once parliament had been purged and the threat of a Royalist-Presbyterian treaty had been averted, the Grandees could dispense with Leveller assistance. Furthermore, by purging rather than dissolving the House, the Grandees had regained the support of the parliamentary Independents who had feared the loss of their seats.

The second *Agreement of the People* was a radical document but showed signs of Leveller concessions to the Independents on the committee. The suggested franchise, though broader than that favoured by Ireton at Putney, explicitly excluded wage-earners; in addition, there was to be a Council of State to control affairs between meetings of parliament. The former may have been simply the clarification of a position the Levellers had always held, though they had never stated it as bluntly as this; the Council of State, on the other hand, can hardly have met with their wholehearted approval for they had always opposed any executive authority not

74

obviously responsible to the will of 'the people'. But the individual rights laid down in the first *Agreement* were still there, as well as the main provisions of the Leveller programme for economic and legal reform—including the controversial demand for tithe abolition.

In the Council of Officers, the new *Agreement* foundered, surprisingly, on the question of religious toleration. The Independents, though strongly opposed to the intolerance of the Presbyterian system, did not want the state to abdicate *all* its religious authority. Ireton drew a distinction between compulsion and restriction. No man, he argued, should be coerced into a set of religious beliefs his conscience would not allow him to accept, but the state should keep the power to restrain those practising idolatry (Roman Catholics) or atheism. The Levellers would not accept this limitation, as Lilburne, Overton and Wildman, who attended these debates in Whitehall, made clear. After angry scenes, in which Lilburne challenged his opponents to single combat, the Levellers withdrew in disgust and published their own unadulterated *Agreement*. The officers' version, heavily amended throughout, was eventually presented to the Commons on 20 January 1649, but as that was the day on which the king's trial began it was, predictably, shelved. The Grandees were content.

The Levellers had suffered a shattering defeat. Invited into the highest councils when the Grandees were weak, they were discarded once their usefulness had passed. The break came over religious toleration, but any other issue would have done as well; Grandees and Levellers were poles apart in their political thinking and their uneasy alliance was unlikely to last any longer than was convenient for the officers. All hope of a constitutional settlement before the removal of the king, the point on which the Levellers had taken their stand, vanished as Cromwell and Ireton, brushing aside the protests of royalists, Presbyterians and Levellers alike, made preparations for a special court to try Charles. The party leadership was in disarray. Lilburne, denouncing the Independents as 'a pack of dissembling, juggling knaves', went north to collect the reparations that had at last been voted to him. Though his absence at this juncture ensured silence on the left throughout the period of the king's trial and execution, it should probably be put down to disappointment rather than sudden desertion for personal gain. Wildman moved off to the profits of land speculation, pursued by the recriminations of his comrades. Even Walwyn, the most philosophical of the Levellers, retired temporarily. As the tragedy of Charles I drew to its close, the Leveller party, whose members had been the first to suggest that a king might be brought to account like other men, moved into the shadows.

ENGLAND'S NEW CHAINS DISCOVERED

Charles I was beheaded on 30 January 1649 and shortly afterwards the Rump passed resolutions that both the House of Lords and the monarchy should be abolished. The country was to be ruled by a Council of State—little more than a committee of the purged Parliament—and the Rump itself. The worst fears of the Levellers had been realised. The king had been removed and in his place, vested with all the authority formerly exercised by the crown in parliament, stood a small Independent oligarchy which, for all its pious lip-service to the democratic principle 'that the people are under God the original of all just power' (4 January 1649), was totally unrepresentative and uncontrolled. The Leveller vision of a constitution based on the sovereignty of the people, so fresh only a little while ago, faded before a nominated Council of State and a mere remnant of the Long Parliament elected in 1640.

The only possible check on the power of the Rump was the army and for the moment, whatever differences might lie beneath the surface, Grandees and parliamentarians could not afford disunity. Together they had tried and executed an anointed king; together they had to face the consequences. Everywhere there was opposition to the new republic. At home royalists and Presbyterians, shocked by Charles's death, eyed each other speculatively, already contemplating the alliance that eventually led to the Restoration of 1660. Abroad a shudder ran through the courts of Europe. The United Provinces promptly recognised Charles II; France forbade the import of English draperies and allowed her privateers to plunder English shipping; even in Russia merchants found themselves imprisoned and their goods confiscated. Closer at hand the traditional trouble spots threatened danger. In Scotland Charles II was proclaimed king six days after the death of his father; in Ireland a confused civil war continued, with a Royalist–Catholic alliance making headway against the parliamentary interest. So for the time being the military and civil groups acted as one, their unity enhanced and symbolised by Cromwell who, as an M.P., the most influential officer in the army and the key figure in the Council of State, was a constant reminder that power lay ultimately with the sword.

The Levellers greeted the New Year in a spirit of despondency. Even the mercurial Lilburne reflected the apathy of the moment: 'I confess I was in a kind of deep muse with myself, what to do with myself; being like an old weather-beaten ship that would fain be in some harbour of ease and rest'. For a while after his return from the north he considered giving up politics altogether to devote himself to his long-suffering wife and children. The republican régime offered him a post under the new administration, but he refused. Though the money would have been welcome, for he could not decide what trade to follow and was living on capital, he had no intention of giving moral support to 'so unjust and illegal a fabric as . . . an everlasting Parliament purged twice by force of arms'; nor could he bring himself to take a salary paid for by 'the sweat of poor people's brows'. He retired to the Leveller stronghold of Southwark and looked for more honest work. With the *Agreement of the People* amended and shelved, its conservative opponents firmly established in the seat of government, and its leader contemplating a complete withdrawal from politics, the Leveller party appeared to be dead.

Appearances were deceptive. The Levellers had been out-manoeuvred and defeated; they were never again to attain the position of influence they had enjoyed at Windsor. But they still had their party organisation and were, in fact, on the brink of a revival which was to keep their hopes alive—and their opponents anxious—for most of the year. Indeed, the new government found it necessary to deal with this internal threat before it turned to the pressing Irish problem.

Lilburne's return to the political scene was a characteristically generous gesture. He had already criticised, and refused a seat on, the High Court that had condemned the King, on the grounds that it was an arbitrary tribunal having no basis in law. Now he claimed that the special court set up on 3 February to try five royalist peers captured during the second Civil War was equally illegal. Created by a 'mock parliament' no longer representative of anyone but itself, the new High Court was, in Lilburne's eyes, an illegal body endangering the liberty of every subject. He offered advice to the prisoners, sent them legal books and developed a genuine admiration for 'stout Capel', who stood up for his rights in true Lilburnian fashion. 'Where is my jury?' Lord Capel demanded, looking round the tribunal at the enemies who were both judge and jury. 'I hope you will not deny me the benefit of the Law, which you pretend you have fought this seven years to maintain.' His defence was noble but unavailing. The death sentences that followed confirmed Lilburne's opinion of the 'abominable wickedness' of the court and the government it represented.

Meanwhile the Levellers again looked to the army; here lay both the strength and the weakness of the Grandees. In mid-February, a petition containing a number of inflammatory demands was circulated through the ranks. Martial law came under fire 'as being too severe and tyrannous for an army of freeborn Englishmen'; the men asked that the army should be relieved of such police duties as 'seizing upon unlicensed books or printing presses'; and, most significant of all, it was requested that the Council of the Army should resume its sittings along the democratic lines agreed upon in the *Solemn Engagement*. Idle soldiers, it seemed, were once more turning to politics.

The response of the Grandees was sharp and immediate. Cromwell and his colleagues had not forgotten how near they had come to losing control of the army in the summer and autumn of 1647; nor had they forgotten that a firm stand at Putney and Ware had brought the ranks to heel. This time they did not intend to give the agitation the chance to gather impetus. On 22 February an order of the day was issued forbidding meetings for the discussion of petitions and stating that all complaints should in future be channelled through the officers of the regiment. In addition, it was made clear that civilians stirring up trouble in the army would not be tolerated and it was even suggested that they should be subject to martial, rather than civil, law. 'We can hang twenty before they will hang one', said Colonel Hewson, always one of the more belligerent officers.

It was this action on the part of the officers' council that provoked Lilburne to resume wholehearted political agitation. Four days after the obnoxious order, he reappeared at the bar of the House of Commons to present *England's New Chains Discovered*, a paper containing a summary of Leveller constitutional ideas and, more important, a fierce denunciation of the leaders of the army and the Council of State.

The constitutional proposals are interesting primarily as an illustration of Leveller hostility to any powerful executive. In the compromise second *Agreement*, worked out with the Independents, they had accepted a Council of State to act between biennial parliaments. The Council of State found no place in the new scheme. Lilburne now suggested that parliament should be annual and that administration between sittings should be in the hands of a committee of M.P.s 'limited and bounded with express instructions, and accountable to the next session'. Plainly the further Leveller dreams receded, the more remote from reality their plans became. With annual parliaments and a temporary executive bound hand and foot, continuity of government policy would have become a near impossibility. Yet this fear of a strong central authority was part of the Levellers' legacy to the English left; the Chartists, too, called for annual parliaments.

The main purpose of the paper, however, was to attack the Grandees for their betrayal of the cause. Where was the liberty for which the army had fought? All around Lilburne saw the symptoms of a new tyranny: arbitrary courts trying men without juries; a press censorship as vigorous as in the days of the bishops; the suppression of honest soldiers' petitions: here indeed was 'the vilest and basest bondage that ever English men groan'd under'.

Lilburne's tone towards the Rump itself was moderate and respectful. It is not difficult to see that he hoped to drive a wedge between parliament and the army by condemning the officers as unscrupulous schemers and appealing to the Rump as the last guardian of liberty. Later, when outside pressures were less acute and soldiers and civilians had had time to fall out with each other, this tactic might have enjoyed some success; in the meantime it was excessively optimistic to imagine that a body recently purged by Colonel Pride would dismiss the officers who had put it in power and abolish the Council of State it had only just appointed.

England's New Chains was not addressed merely to the Rump; it marked the beginning of a fresh campaign in the country at large and was immediately published in *The Moderate*. To engage the attention of the man in the street, Lilburne included the main points of the Leveller social and economic programme—items with a special relevance in yet another winter of food shortage, rising prices and unemployment. For the army there was the demand that the Rump should deal with arrears of pay and set up a committee to investigate grievances among the men. Once again the Leveller were opening up on a broad front.

The soldiers responded first. On 1 March eight troopers presented a Leveller-inspired petitition to Fairfax, demanding restoration of the right to petition freely; Overton wrote it and arranged for it publication. The officers' reaction was predictable. The eight men were arrested and after three had apologised and been pardoned the remainder were court-martialled. Told they deserved death they were instead cashiered, suffering a degrading ceremony at the head of their regiments before being taken off to be fêted as heroes at one of the Leveller taverns.

There were other signs of the Leveller offensive. Lilburne was refurbishing the party machine and sending out agents to encourage the non-payment of taxes; the March issues of *The Moderate* grew increasingly revolutionary in tone; and it was reported from Hitchin that troopers had demonstrated in the market-place in favour of the Leveller programme. The new attack from the left was gaining momentum. But it was not as dangerous as it looked. To undermine the authority of the Council of State the Levellers had to destroy the discipline of the army and this was no easy task after the Grandees' resolute stand at Ware. Individual soldiers were prepared to flaunt sea-green ribbons and one or two regiments were unreliable, as the disturbances of April and May were to prove, but on the whole the army remained loyal to Cromwell. The ease with which the scattered and ineffective outbreaks were put down adequately illustrates the firm grip the officers maintained.

The Leveller leaders were more aware of their weakness than their enemies. Following the cashiering of the five troopers, Overton produced his most bitter pamphlet, the picturesquely named *The Hunting of the Foxes from Newmarket and Triploe Heaths to Whitehall, by five small Beagles (late of the Army)* [**doc. 9**]. This class-conscious assault on the Grandees (the Foxes), allegedly written by the disgraced soldiers (the Beagles), reflected the desperation and disillusionment of a party that had little left to lose. Savage with irony and invective, *The Hunting of the Foxes* was a distorted history of the last two years, in which Cromwell and Ireton were the hypocritical villains and the ordinary soldiers the heroes. The officers had betrayed the cause from the beginning. While the rank and file had sought genuine reform, Cromwell and his colleagues had been engaged in a monstrous conspiracy to take over the government themselves. Lies and deceits had duped the honest soldiers; by their 'Machiavellian practices' the Grandees had climbed to power on the shoulders of men they considered mere 'mercenary slaves'. Every charge—truth, half-truth and blatant falsehood—that could be levied was pressed into service. 'Was there ever a generation of men so apostate, so false, so perjured as these?'

The Levellers were burning their boats. *The Hunting of the Foxes* was at once a frenzied cry to the ordinary soldiers to bestir themselves before it was too late and a challenge to the Grandees to do their worst: there could be no rapprochement with the new rulers after this. As if to show that Overton's work was not the outburst of an isolated individual but part of a planned campaign, Lilburne followed it up with *The Second Part of England's New Chains Discovered*, an equally strident paper supported by many signatures and presented to the Commons on 24 March. Again the Grandees' record was held up for contempt to prove the Leveller thesis that they had never intended to keep any of the engagements made with their men; again they were charged with a long-term plot to erect a military despotism. Lilburne's solution was simple: the Rump, the last poor vestige of legal authority, should adopt the *Agreement of the People* and then dissolve itself; the democratic Council of the Army should be restored to wrest control from the 'faction of officers'. If this did not happen, Lilburne implied, the people might take matters into their own hands. The threat of rebellion was scarcely veiled.

The Levellers can hardly have expected to get away with such outspoken propaganda; indeed, it is possible that they hoped to provoke a vigorous repression which would amply illustrate the charges they made. Certainly Cromwell's patience was exhausted. He was indifferent to personal criticism, but was acutely aware of the problems facing the Commonwealth and could not allow the Levellers to divide the army against itself. One last effort was made to persuade Lilburne to take a post under the administration and when this was refused the government struck. The Rump carried a resolution that the authors of *The Second Part of England's New Chains* were guilty of high treason for attempting to breed mutiny in the army and should be punished accordingly. In the early hours of the day following, four strong detachments of troops, each numbering between one and two hundred men, clattered through the deserted streets to arrest Lilburne, Overton, Walwyn and Thomas Prince. The time of day and the strength of the force deployed were a tribute to the popularity of the prisoners; the inclusion of Walwyn, who had played no part in Leveller activities since the breakdown of the negotiations at Whitehall, suggests a determination to crush the whole group once for all.

Lilburne, well versed in the matter of arrests, was soon on friendly terms with the officer in charge of his escort and took him off for a drink at a nearby tavern. Overton had a less genial man to deal with, one Lieutenant-Colonel Axtell. Convinced by the crowded conditions of Overton's lodgings that he had run his man to earth in a brothel, he abused his prisoner, insulted other members of the household, and arrested a trooper, who was in bed with his wife, for fornication. In his subsequent account of the affair, Overton made full play with Axtell's blundering behaviour, asking whether the new régime had taken over control of husbands, wives and beds as well as laws, king and parliament.

Late in the afternoon the four men were called individually before the Council of State. Lilburne made the most of the occasion. He kept his hat on until he recognised certain members of parliament and then removed it ostentatiously. Questioned about his part in the offending pamphlet, he claimed that the Council had no right to try him; parliament could make the law but having no executive powers could hardly delegate them to a council. Finding the whole episode reminiscent of his experiences before Star Chamber, he refused to answer any questions. His fellow prisoners did likewise.

After each had made two abortive appearances before the Council, the Levellers were put in an anteroom while their case was debated. Lilburne decided to eavesdrop at the keyhole and—according to his later account—caught Cromwell in aggressive mood. Thumping his fist on the table, he stormed: 'I tell you, sir, you have no other way to deal with these men but to break them in pieces; . . . if you do not break them, they will break you.' The Council sat till midnight and then decreed that the prisoners should be committed to the Tower—'my old and contented lodging', as Lilburne remarked with an unwonted flash of humour.

As the prison doors closed on him yet again, Lilburne could reflect with satisfaction that in spite of the setback at Whitehall he and his party had once more gravitated to the centre of the political arena: Cromwell's anger during the Council debate was a measure of their success. Nevertheless, the Grandees were exaggerating the real importance of the Levellers and their repressive action should be seen in the wider context of the urgent political and economic problems to be dealt with. The Council of State, beset at home and abroad, could not afford trouble in either London or the army; small wonder they moved swiftly against the Levellers who, though struggling on the downward path, still had influence in both. It remained to be seen how long Lilburne, once more playing the familiar rôle of martyr, could enable his party to survive the counterrevolution now in progress.

5 Death of the Party

BURFORD

The imprisonment of the party leaders evoked a sharp response in London. Several petitions demanding a fair trial were presented to the Commons, one containing ten thousand signatures. A demonstration staged by hundreds of women—women were always prominent in Leveller agitation—led to a rebuke from the Speaker, who told them they were meddling with matters they could not understand. This ill-advised intervention brought a spirited retort from the women, who drew up a petition claiming a measure of equality of the sexes: 'Since we are assured of our creation in the image of God, of an interest in Christ equal unto men . . . Have we not an equal interest with the men of this nation in their liberties and securities . . .?' Even in decline, the Levellers were breaking new ground.

Outwardly, in spite of its setbacks, the party exhibited remarkable virility; beneath the surface there were ominous hints of disintegration. The Fifth Monarchists, believing Christ's Second Coming to be imminent, were already active and tended to draw off Leveller support. Several Independent congregations in London, hitherto constant allies, announced not merely withdrawal of sympathy but outright opposition. Shocked by what they took to be evidence of scepticism and agnosticism in Leveller thought, they first disassociated themselves from *The Second Part of England's New Chains* and then fiercely attacked the party in general and Walwyn in particular in *Walwyn's Wiles*. Now they had acquired their long sought toleration, the Independent congregations were prepared to make their peace with the new régime.

The arrest of Lilburne and his colleagues did not unduly handicap the Leveller campaign. A situation was developing in the army akin to that before the mutiny of 1647 and the Levellers were quick to appreciate the opportunity: it must have occurred to some of them

hat this might well be their last chance. It had been decided to send
an army to Ireland under Comwell's command. Men volunteering
for service were to receive three months' pay and debentures
covering their arrears; those who refused were to be dismissed
without any guarantees. Not surprisingly, many soldiers recalled
the promises of the *Solemn Engagement*. The Grandees, who had
shown such concern for prior engagements at Putney when it had
suited them, had shorter memories.

The Levellers urged resistance. *The English Soldier's Standard*,
probably by Walwyn, called for the reconstruction of the General
Council of the Army and the acceptance of an Agreement of the
People. This was predictable. Less obvious, and more interesting,
was the appearance of Leveller opposition to a reconquest of Ireland
on ethical grounds. During the second Civil War Walwyn had discussed the horror of war and the need of the individual conscience
to know the cause was just. Now he challenged the righteousness of
the cause. A pamphlet was circulated among the troops questioning
England's right to conquer Ireland and putting forward a plan for
an independent Irish state (**13**). Although no copy of it survives, this
pamphlet may be considered one of the Levellers' more important
contributions. It shows not only that they had emancipated themselves from the Puritan bigotry which identified Irish Roman
Catholics as debased savages in league with the devil, but also their
recognition of human rights transcending the narrow limits of
nationalism.

Economics rather than ethics led to the first open defiance of the
Grandees. A troop of horse barricaded itself in the Bull Inn at
Bishopsgate and refused to stir until its arrears had been met. Only
when Fairfax and Cromwell arrived in person did they surrender.
The Grandees took a serious view of this disaffection and at the
subsequent court-martial six troopers were sentenced to death.
Eventually five were reprieved, but Robert Lockyer, a Leveller
agitator who had been prominent at Ware, faced a firing squad in
front of St Paul's—an execution reflecting the officers' determination to crush any mutiny at its outset. For Lockyer's funeral the
Levellers organised another impressive demonstration, with both
soldiers and civilians following the coffin.

Lockyer's death served as the overture to the Levellers' last major
attempt to destroy the discipline of the New Model. On 1 May
Lilburne, Walwyn, Overton and Prince published the final version

of the *Agreement of the People* [**doc. 4**], its avowed purpose being to 'abolish all arbitrary power . . . and remove all known grievances'. Shortly afterwards six regiments elected new agitators and one of them, Colonel Scroop's cavalry, already on the way to Ireland, halted at Salisbury and refused to continue the march. In Oxfordshire William Thompson, an aggressive Leveller, published *England's Standard Advanced*, calling for a full-scale revolt; he himself set an example by collecting together a number of disaffected troops at Banbury. News spread of unrest elsewhere, including a Leveller rally at Aylesbury.

The Grandees acted swiftly. The Leveller prisoners were more rigorously confined in the Tower. A review of their troops was held in Hyde Park, at which Fairfax and Cromwell promised that those not wishing to go to Ireland should have their arrears dealt with as promptly as those who volunteered. The loyalty of their own men thus assured—concessions had been necessary for there had been disturbing signs of sea-green ribbons in Hyde Park—the general set off westwards to prevent a projected junction of the units in revolt.

They overtook the main body of Levellers, some 1200 men, at midnight in the Cotswold town of Burford. There was a little desultory fighting, but the bulk of the mutineers, surprised in their beds by superior numbers, dispersed or surrendered. Thompson escaped, to be eventually hunted down and killed after refusing quarter in a wood near Wellingborough. Three hundred and forty prisoners were taken and shut up in Burford Church. Three days later, after all had been condemned to death by court-martial, three men were shot in the churchyard, the remainder watching from the leads of the church. The rebels had been in touch with the generals before they reached Burford and one sympathetic account claims that they were lulled into a false sense of security by promises from Cromwell that they would not be attacked while negotiations continued. This may have been so, but with Cromwell in the mood described by Lilburne at his recent appearance before the Council of State it is unlikely that he would have considered himself bound by assurances given to mutineers in arms.

The Cause had failed again; there was black despair at the Whalebone Tavern. Lilburne, whose summer was blighted by the death of his two sons from smallpox, showed the essential weakness of his party in *An Impeachment of High Treason against Oliver Cromwell and his son-in-law Henry Ireton.* Here, after a vehement assault on the Grandees, he suggested there might be common ground between Levellers and royalists if Prince Charles would accept the Agreement. The desperation that led to overtures to royalists reached a climax in *The Remonstrance of the Free People of England*, an inflammatory petition calling unambiguously for armed rebellion. Although the Levellers claimed the remarkable number of 98,064 signatures to this paper, its extreme language was a symptom of impotence rather than strength. It is easier to agree with Frank, who calls it 'the death rattle of the Leveller party' (**14**), than Brailsford, who uses it as evidence that 'in the autumn of 1649 it [the Leveller party] reached the height of its influence and prestige' (**13**).

However, there was a revival of sorts at this time, though it never came near to success and served only to convince the Council of State of the need to suppress the Levellers completely. A dispute between the lead miners of Derbyshire, many of whom were small masters in decline, and the Earl of Rutland temporarily provided the party with a fresh source of support; but the miners' resolution failed when troops were sent to disarm them. In Oxford, at the instigation of another Lilburne pamphlet, a regiment of foot elected new representatives, secured its officers in New College and demanded the restoration of the democratic Council of the Army. Lacking leadership, they were soon outmanoeuvred and put down; two more soldiers were shot. The last attempt to suborn the army had foundered.

These disturbances and rumours of others were enough for the Council of State. Fearful of collaboration between Levellers and royalists, and aware that the harvest had failed yet again, the government turned to general repression. Strict orders were given for the arrest of all Leveller troublemakers. In September a fierce licensing act silenced *The Moderate*. Finally, and with some trepidation, the Council of State tackled the man who more than anyone else kept Leveller hopes alive—John Lilburne. Preparations were begun for his trial on a charge of treason.

The wheel had turned full circle. The Leveller party was about to expire as it had been born: in a blaze of publicity attendant upon a personal appearance of its extraordinary leader.

DISINTEGRATION

Lilburne's trial in the Guildhall provided the excuse for the last mass Leveller demonstration. Backed by a crowd of sympathisers crushed into the hall and many others listening at the open doors, Lilburne produced a display of legalistic virtuosity that enabled him to take the initiative and hold it throughout the trial. He was greatly helped by the judges who, though outraged and dismayed by the procedural quibbles with which he stalled the court at every turn, were so anxious to let the public see he was being given a fair trial that they allowed themselves to be inveigled into trivialities. As a result the whole affair came near to ridicule. Conscious of his audience throughout, Lilburne rebuked the attorney-general for whispering 'in hugger-mugger' with the judges, had a shouting match with the bench, and took complete charge of the proceedings when he appealed to his supporters to be a little quieter as he could not hear the indictment being read.

The charge against him had been brought under a new Treason Act, passed during the tension surrounding the disturbances at Burford. The Act's broad and potentially tyrannical definition of treason made it particularly vulnerable to Lilburne's methods and he had no difficulty in donning the mantle of martyrdom on behalf of traditional English liberties. The pamphlets brought as evidence against him, however, fell firmly within its scope and Lilburne had little alternative but to run for legal loopholes and proclaim the injustice of the act. When he made his final plea to the jury, he asserted that they were judges of law as well as fact—a startling claim, in accord with Leveller thinking, which would have given the jurymen the right to ignore laws they found obnoxious.

Whichever part of his performance impressed them, the jury returned a verdict of 'not guilty' and shouts of triumph, lasting half an hour, filled the close-packed hall. Lilburne was returned to the Tower amidst the acclamations of the soldiers escorting him as well as the citizens of London. That night bonfires blazed in the streets and church bells pealed their tribute; later, when he and the other leaders were eventually released, a day of thanksgiving was appointed and the party struck a medal in his honour.

London had never shown its affection for Lilburne more clearly, yet, paradoxically, the triumph of his acquittal coincided with the end of his party; perhaps the warmth of his reception was influenced by the realisation that this might be the last occasion to demonstrate it. No doubt links were maintained in the taverns and 'gathered' congregations, and one or two petitions were organised in the 1650s, notably in 1653 when Lilburne was once more on trial for his life; but by the end of 1649 the party had lost its coherence and was dead as a political force.

The immediate causes of the collapse are not hard to find. No party can survive indefinitely in the face of continual defeat and the history of the Levellers contained nothing but setbacks since the auspicious negotiations at Windsor in 1648. The suppression of the mutiny at Burford, followed by the strict precautionary measures of the autumn, revealed the stability of the Council of State and the relative weakness of the Levellers. Lilburne's success at the Guild-hall may have given the Independent régime red faces, but it did not alter the fundamental balance of power within the state. Once the Levellers had failed to shake the loyalty of the army, their ultimate oblivion was assured. Moreover, by 1650 the Scottish threat was being resurrected north of the border: the alliance of Prince Charles with the Covenanters heralded a new civil war. As in 1648 the Levellers rallied to the government; they knew better than to embarrass the Independents by the encouragement of a Royalist–Presbyterian coalition. But this time a period of stagnation was fatal. Already disheartened, the remnants of the party withered away.

Lilburne had not yet finished his personal crusade against authority, but the battles still to be fought were those of an incorrigible individualist not a party leader. A period of relative calm followed his aquittal and he took up the trade of soap-boiling. He could not remain out of trouble for long, however. In 1650, once again associated with Wildman, he gave moral support and legal advice to the commoners of Epworth in Lincolnshire, who were opposing the enclosure of land for a fen drainage scheme. Then, in 1652, a personal vendetta of long standing with Sir Arthur Haslerig, a powerful neighbour of his in County Durham, came to a head in a series of defamatory attacks from Lilburne. The Rump, possibly worried at signs of increasing activity on his part or still harbouring resentment at his escape in 1649, took the opportunity offered by these libels on one of its most prominent members to crush him. It passed a monstrous sentence: a fine of £7,000 and banishment for life, together with the threat of death as a felon if he should return

D

to the country. The tyranny the Levellers had feared had become a reality.

In exile in the Low Countries, Lilburne met, and liked, several royalists. Though he later denied it vehemently, it is possible that he negotiated for a Royalist–Leveller alliance; certainly his experiences of a republic had convinced him of the advantages of a constitutional monarchy. By 1653 he could stand exile no more and after the dissolution of the Rump he returned to England, without a safe-conduct but promising to live 'quietly and submissively'. He was arrested immediately and put on trial for his life under the Rump's vicious sentence. For a brief moment he swam back into the public eye. Petitions for his release came from several Leveller strongholds. His trial at the Old Bailey had much in common with his earlier appearance at the Guildhall—crowds of supporters, exasperated judges, and a histrionic performance from the central figure. Eventually, after a long deliberation, the jury found him 'Not guilty of any crime worthy of death'. But Lilburne was not released. Moved from prison to prison, he slowly deteriorated in health, and in 1657, at the age of forty-three, he died. Sad and disillusioned though he was, he found tranquillity in his last years when the turbulent arrogance of his religious faith softened to the humility and mysticism of the Quaker creed.

The other leaders, with the exception of Wildman, who plotted his conspiratorial way until the Revolution of 1688, had little more to say. Walwyn retired to the bosom of his large family; Overton linked himself with the royalists in the 1650s and vanished from view in 1663 after being imprisoned for criticism of the Restoration government; Sexby, too, worked with the royalists and died in prison in 1658.

What of the rank and file, the men Lilburne described as 'the hobnails, clouted shoes, the private soldiers, the leather and woollen aprons, and the laborious and industrious people of England'? Though defeated and disconsolate, they remained combustible political material. They still had their grievances, perhaps made more dangerous by their visions of what might have been, and, above all, they still had their religious faith. This dedicated Puritanism had already led them to become Levellers; now it took many of their number towards the Fifth Monarchists and Quakers.

The Fifth Monarchists, believing the Second Coming to be imminent, urged the erection of a theocracy of 'saints' to purge society of sin and 'make straight the way of the Lord'. The poor need no longer wait for eternal bliss; the Kingdom of God was at hand and with His help they would 'put down the mighty from their seat'. Their revolutionary programme, particularly their plans for tithe abolition and law reform, differed little from the Levellers'. The authoritarian way in which these changes were to be enforced, though wholly alien to Leveller thinking, may have had a certain appeal for men disillusioned by the response of 'the people' to their previous idealistic designs. The Fifth Monarchists' day was to come in 1653 when they nearly took control of the Barebones Parliament.

The first Quakers shared the Fifth Monarchists' hostility to the injustice of a sinful society, and they, too, believed in the approaching Millenium. But here the similarities ended. The Quakers rejected predestination, emphasising instead the 'inner light'—direct spiritual communion with God—available to 'every man that cometh into the world'. Their duty was to convince all men of the possibilities within them and to create a pure Christian community based on the teachings of the primitive church. They believed passionately in equality, symbolised by their refusal to remove their hats as a mark of respect, and this led them to a comprehensive indictment of the hierarchical society in which they lived. They rejected the ceremonial of a 'hireling ministry' and hence frequently refused to pay the tithes that supported it. Thus they had a good deal of common ground with the Levellers and many of the latter hastened to the spiritual haven provided by the Society of Friends when their own cause collapsed. Not surprisingly, for initially the Friends were not the pacifists they later became, the traditional social order turned on the Quakers as ruthlessly as it had on the Levellers (**26, 29**).

So the party disintegrated. Soldiers and artisans who had for a short while glimpsed and influenced the doings in the corridors of power faded into the obscurity whence they had come. Their radical ideal, with all its shortcomings, remained shrouded for another century and a half.

Part Three

ASSESSMENT

6 Why did the Levellers fail?

For two years the Leveller party was a major factor in politics and at one point—in May 1647, at Newmarket—it seemed about to seize control of the revolution altogether. But it failed. Outmanoeuvred on the debating floor and crushed in the field, it collapsed as dramatically as it had grown. At the time, contemporaries thought the Levellers had a good chance of success and hoped or feared accordingly. In retrospect, we can see that their importance was overestimated. The reasons for their failure were numerous and overwhelming.

In the first place, the strength of the Levellers was something of an illusion. It is true that they exerted pressure on the Independents and outlined a course of action much of which was ultimately followed. Opposition to disbandment, the capture of London in 1647, the purge of parliament, the death of the king, and the abolition of monarchy and Lords—all originated with the Levellers. But there were other pressures forcing the Grandees to the left. The duplicity of the king, the interference of the Scots and the reactionary policies of the English Presbyterians acted just as potently, and it is probable that the Independents would have been forced by circumstances to adopt these expedients anyway. In fact, the Levellers were not as strong as they looked. Apart from the initial army revolt of 1647, the Levellers never dictated events; their influence grew or diminished according to the prevailing political situation. Thus, in 1648, just before Pride's Purge, when the Grandees wanted allies, the Levellers appeared powerful; at Ware and Burford, when the Grandees wanted to exert their authority, the party's real weaknesses were exposed.

The Levellers flourished in the chronic political instability and economic hardship of the years 1647–49. The negotiating quadrilateral of King, Presbyterians, Scots and Grandees and the series of disastrous harvests together formed ideal conditions for radical agitation. But these did not last. The rule of the Rump after the death of the king may have been arbitrary and corrupt, but it provided efficient government, to which even the Venetian ambassador bore witness. Moreover, the distress consequent upon economic hardship diminished in the early 1650s. The purchasing power of wages rose sharply and culminated in 'the two most prosperous years of the century [1653–55]'. (**10**).

There were fundamental weaknesses in the Leveller programme. It demanded at once too little and too much. Too little in that it offered real advantages to only a small proportion of the population; too much in that it used such revolutionary language and was aimed in so many directions that all vested interests clung together for protection. The men who stood to gain were the lower-middle classes, the declining craftsmen and the small landowners. There was not much to interest the vast majority of poorer people. Tithe abolition had an obvious appeal and some of the proposed social legislation would have helped them. But wage-earners, servants and paupers were expressly excluded from the suffrage; the sanctity of property was to be maintained, as the leaders reiterated in the face of constant misrepresentation; and although they occasionally talked of doing away with 'base tenures' (copyholds) the Levellers never established this as a major part of their platform and the final *Agreement of the People* made no mention of agrarian problems at all. Yet, while turning their backs on the mass of the rural population, the Levellers showed little discretion in their choice of enemies. Landowners, merchants, lawyers, army officers, clerics—all at one time or another were antagonised by barbed attacks and lent their support to the reaction that destroyed the party.

In any case, the Levellers tended to be preoccupied with constitutional theories which were too subtle for popular consumption. The first *Agreement* concentrated solely on political theory and the debates at Putney can have meant little to the ordinary people. Leveller strength rested in the main on their plans for economic reform and army discontent over pay. But the Grandees steadily eroded this support by taking over key parts of their programme. They backed demands for pay throughout the period and shortly before leaving for Ireland in 1649 petitioned the Rump to consider some reform of tithes and the law. Once deprived of the credit for such proposals, the Levellers' purely constitutional platform would not go far.

Nor did the Levellers enjoy the unity they needed to achieve greater success. Several Independent congregations withdrew their support when religious toleration arrived with the establishment of the Commonwealth. Two pamphlets from Buckinghamshire went further in their demands for economic equality than any produced by the official leadership and it is possible to infer some dissatisfaction on the part of the Chiltern Levellers. The soldiers did not look far beyond their own pay grievances and only seemed interested in civilian troubles when it suited them. Such disparate aims were reflected in the lack of coordination at times of crisis. A large body of weavers was to have attended the rendezvous at Ware to show solidarity with the troops: it did not turn up. The mutiny involving Lockyer was a spontaneous protest quite unconnected with any calculated plan. The revolt put down at Burford was more serious, but attempts to link this with unrest elsewhere were singularly ineffective. In September 1649, 98,064 people apparently signed Lilburne's *Remonstrance*, yet the last miserable mutiny at Oxford in the same month gained no help at all, though the mutineers had been led to believe that thousands of supporters would flock in from the Midlands. It is a doleful commentary on the Levellers' talent for organisation that their most notable successes were the demonstrations at the funerals of their dead heroes.

The Levellers' real failure was in the army. The measure of importance they achieved depended almost entirely on their influence in the New Model; while Lilburne's 'seditious scribblings' held sway amongst the ordinary soldiers, he and his colleagues could never be ignored by the Independents. But from an early stage Cromwell discovered that the respect for traditional social leadership, backed by the spirit of loyalty created in war, was more potent than the revolutionary propaganda permeating the ranks. The Grandees had their moments of doubt—the Leveller martyrs at Ware and Burford knew how to die—but, once they had absorbed the shock of the initial agitation, they steadily resumed control and never lost it again. It is in this context that one sees the full significance of Rainsborough's untimely death. Courageous, principled, and among the ablest commanders in the New Model, he was the one officer who might have diverted the loyalties of the men into more radical paths (**50**).

In the last analysis, the Levellers' failure was due to their inability to stir the lower classes to action on their own behalf. This may be explained partly by the shortcomings in their programme and partly by the simple physical problems of communication in the seventeenth century. But even if these had been overcome, it is very doubtful whether the supporters needed would have been forthcoming. The vast bulk of the population was socially conservative and politically apathetic. The Civil War itself, whatever the principles at stake, had been an internecine struggle among the propertied classes. The ordinary people had on the whole been disinterested spectators whose main hope was to avoid impressment by one side or the other—an attitude best expressed by the neutralist 'Clubmen', who banded together to keep both adversaries out of their area. The Levellers did their best to counteract this political illiteracy with their petitions, designed to inform and educate as well as to elicit immediate support, but the task was too great. In London and the army, where unique conditions prevailed, they achieved temporary success; elsewhere the Leveller dream was shared by too few and feared by too many.

7 In Perspective

The seventeenth century was a time of crisis. Historians disagree when they try to explain exactly what was happening, but whether they use Marxist vocabulary and talk of the transition from a feudal to a capitalist economy, or whether they postulate a clash between 'Court' and 'Country', there is a measure of accord over the basic premise: there was an economic and political crisis, not only in England but in western Europe as a whole (**6**). Moreover, the intellectual temper was changing. Scientists were abandoning medieval concepts and seeking the truth through the empirical collection of data; philosophers like Descartes and Hobbes, admiring the rigorous discipline of mathematics, turned more and more to systematic analysis to solve their problems. Everywhere the old certainties were giving ground before the spirit of reason and experiment.

The Civil War and all that followed was a manifestation of this general crisis in England, and within this upheaval one of the most important themes was the questioning of traditional authority. English society was authoritarian from top to bottom. The patriarchal pattern set in the family extended itself into all the complex political and social relationships of the state: king and subjects, landowner and tenants, master and servants. Supported by all the weight of custom and religious belief, obedience was inculcated from an early age. The catechism taught by parish priests and learned by all children was explicit: 'My duty is . . . to submit myself to all my governors, teachers, spiritual pastors and masters; to order myself lowly and reverently to all my betters; . . . and to do my duty in that state of life unto which it shall please God to call me' (**35**). Ireton had learnt his lesson well. At Putney he said: 'Honour thy father and mother, and that law doth extend to all that are our governors.' The Levellers, as the most influential of the radical groups of the period, were in the van of the assault on these traditional beliefs.

99

John Lilburne spelt out the Leveller challenge in *The Free Man's Freedom Vindicated*:

> All and every particular and individual man and woman, that ever breathed in the world, are by nature all equal and alike in their power, dignity, authority and majesty, none of them having (by nature) any authority, dominion or magisterial power one over or above another (**35**).

It would be difficult to construct a clearer statement of equality than this. From this basic tenet came the Leveller doctrines of sovereignty of the people, full religious toleration and equality before the law. It even encouraged women to political action, a development threatening the very foundations of the patriarchal family (**6, 32**).

Yet the Levellers were not consistent in their political thinking. Quite apart from their difficulties with the fundamental dilemma that afflicts all political philosophers—the need to reconcile the power of the state with the rights and freedoms of the individual—the Levellers never accepted the full consequences of the creed that men 'are by nature all equal'. Although they used the language of democracy, they were not democrats; Rainsborough spoke of the rights of 'the poorest he' and 'the greatest he', but the party disclaimed the title 'leveller' and denied the franchise to wage-earners, servants and paupers. Reason and emotion drove the Levellers to a veiled vision of modern democracy; the veil was not lifted because they could not disencumber themselves entirely from contemporary social prejudices. Walwyn came nearest to it, but Lilburne never forgot he was a 'gentleman', and the main body of urban followers was as anxious to preserve its decaying superiority over the unfortunates beneath as it was to topple the hierarchy above. Those who had 'lost their birthright' remained second-class citizens.

The Levellers' failure to take their ideas to a logical conclusion was thrown into high relief by the activities of the Diggers, a group of extremists, calling themselves 'the true levellers', who emerged early in 1649. Like the Levellers, their philosophy was rooted in Puritanism. Their leader, Gerrard Winstanley, an unsuccessful cloth merchant from Wigan, shared the Quaker faith in an 'inner light': 'Man', he wrote, 'has a teacher within him and this is the spirit that made the globe and lives in every creature.' In obedience to this spiritual revelation, he propagated a gospel of pure communism. He claimed that all the troubles of man stemmed from private property: 'This particular propriety of mine and thine hath brought in all misery upon people. For, first it hath occasioned people to steal from one another. Secondly, it hath made laws to hang those that did steal.' The solution, he argued, lay in the construction of a society in which equality meant exactly what it said; in which the earth was the 'common treasury' of all. To make a start on his utopian society, Winstanley and a handful of landless enthusiasts encamped themselves on St George's Hill, near Walton-on-Thames, dug up the common land there and planted vegetables. This experiment in communal living stood little chance in an age which had already condemned the more moderate Levellers as anarchists. The local gentry gave the Diggers short shrift: they were fined for trespassing, cattle were turned into their crops, and their houses were pulled down. They survived for a year and then succumbed (**13, 24, 26**).

Leveller thought lacked the stark simplicity of Winstanley's communism; it was at once more complicated and confused, a typical product of an age of transition. Critical of traditional conceptions yet only tentatively feeling their way into the future, the Levellers looked both forwards and back. From the past they resurrected the law of nature and the myth of an ideal Anglo-Saxon society; the former to endow individuals with certain inalienable rights, the latter to castigate the powers and privileges of the ruling classes. But they were forward-looking too. In spite of their belief that power corrupts, the Levellers had an essentially optimistic view of man. All men, they considered, have potentiality and this can only be realised to the full in the free type of society envisaged in the *Agreements of the People*. Just as men must be free to find their eternal salvation, so they must be free to work out their temporal destiny on earth. Only when all unnecessary restrictions—for example, inequality before the law, trading privileges, press censorship and conscription—have been abolished, will the fulfilment of the individual become possible. This inherent optimism, constantly seeking an improving society, was also implicit in other reform proposals they put forward from time to time. Overton advocated free primary education and publicly-maintained infirmaries for the poor, while the last *Agreement* proposed a revision of all legal penalities on humanitarian grounds. Such optimism is the basis of modern democracy (**14**).

The Levellers were individualists, not socialists. When drawing up the *Agreements*, they were primarily interested in preserving the rights of the individual. As representatives of the independent tradesmen and artisans, they sought equality before the law and equality of political rights, not equality of property; their aims were political not economic. They wanted to create a society based on the self-interest of the individuals composing it, and their suspicion of state authority led them to hedge it about with extreme limitations whose absurdity would have been speedily revealed had they ever been put into practice. The final *Agreement of the People* proposed annual parliaments, with executive action between sittings entrusted to a committee of the House. To destroy any possible continuity of power, no member of one parliament was to be eligible to sit in its immediate successor; to remove influences of which the Levellers disapproved and to limit patronage possibilities, no serving military or revenue officers were to sit and no lawyer was to practise in the courts while an M.P. At all times the powers of the House over those it represented were bounded by the rights of the individual guaranteed by the 'fundamental law'.

The Levellers' fear of the central executive showed itself in their advocacy of administrative decentralisation; they rebelled consistently against the prevailing tendency for power to concentrate in the hands of the government in London. Taking as their starting point the 'gathered' congregation so many of them knew, they sought to extend the independence of the local community into other fields. The third *Agreement* called for legal decentralisation, including the abolition of the law courts in London and the substitution of regional courts administered by locally elected sheriffs and J.P.s. Likewise, it was proposed that any future army should rest on a local basis. The leading officers would be appointed by parliament, but the men would be raised, equipped and paid by the county, city or town, whose inhabitants would also elect all the officers from regimental commanders downwards. Such a scheme would have removed for ever the fear of a despotism resting on a standing army. This stress on decentralisation again emphasises the individualism of the Leveller philosophy. So that the smaller man would count for something more than he did in the all-embracing state, the Levellers would have given the local community considerable autonomy. 'The England of Lilburne and Walwyn would have been . . . a loose federation of parishes, hundreds and counties' (**13**).

The instability of the Civil War years stimulated intellectual inquiry in general and political thinking in particular. A king had been challenged, defeated and executed; such actions had to be justified. When fighting first broke out, parliament maintained the fiction that the king was being led astray by 'desperate persons'; later, when this myth was difficult to perpetuate in the face of the facts, necessity dictated the development of a theory of parliamentary sovereignty. But on what was this to be based? The near anarchy of the period 1647 to 1649 posed awkward and fundamental questions for the competitors seeking to inherit the crown's power.

Although it was largely obscured at Putney, there was a good deal of common ground between Grandees and Levellers over the vital problem of sovereignty. Both believed that parliament should, in some sense, represent 'the people', and both were anxious to define 'the people' in a restrictive way. The differences lay in approach and in the interests each represented. The Independents were on the defensive; they spoke for the entrenched gentry class which saw parliamentary sovereignty as the guarantor of rights already in existence, the rights of established property protected by Common Law. Locke merely echoed Ireton when he wrote later in the century: 'The great and chief end of men's putting themselves under government . . . is the protection of their property.' The Levellers— with the possible exception of Walwyn, who was always more radical than his colleagues—did not dispute such property rights; indeed, their immediate reaction at Putney when charged with intent to overthrow property was to number the right to property as one of the basic natural rights established by the law of God—another indication that the Levellers were not as far from the Independents' position as the emotional tenor of the debates would suggest. But the Levellers were on the attack; they were the underdogs who, thanks to their experiences in the past, sought guarantees for personal liberties in the future. They may not have been democrats, but they were certainly revolutionaries. By proposing that parliamentary authority should be rooted in a wider cross-section of the population and by joining this extension of the franchise to equal electoral districts, they threatened the whole edifice of landed control. In the absence of a secret ballot landowners would still have exercised considerable influence over the copyholders and tenants-at-will, but rotten boroughs would have vanished and the concept of freehold property as the sole qualification for political

103

power would have suffered a shrewd blow. After they had defeated the Levellers at Burford, Fairfax and Cromwell were honoured with Doctorates of Civil Law at Oxford and entertained at a lavish banquet in the City of London: the men of property knew what they were about.

What, if anything, did the Levellers contribute to posterity? In a sense, very little. Though they said much that sounds modern and democratic, they were a product of the Age of Faith rather than the Age of Reason; their rationalism was a product of God-given conscience rather than new scientific attitudes, their belief in equality was based on a Christian view of the brotherhood of man, not the utilitarian ethics of later centuries. Standing firmly in the tradition of Wycliffe and John Ball, 'they had', in the words of Dr Schenk, 'much more in common with William Langland than with Thomas Paine or Karl Marx' (**26**).

Yet the Levellers were something more than the last abortive flowering of a medieval tradition. Their claim for the freedom and natural rights of the individual, whatever its source, did not disappear entirely. However tenuous, there are connecting links— for example the Quakers—between the radical ideas of the Levellers and kindred groups and the religious nonconformity that was so closely related to social reform and political democracy in the nineteenth century. Furthermore, as the foremost advocates of religious toleration in the period, they encouraged the separation of Church and State that led eventually to the secular society of today, a process of secularisation also stimulated by their anti-clericalism and emphasis on free religious enquiry, both of which weakened traditional dogma and authority.

Professor C. B. Macpherson has suggested another Leveller legacy. In his interesting essay on the Leveller franchise proposals (**23**), he argues that the Levellers subscribed to the theory of 'possessive individualism'; that is, the belief that each individual is essentially the proprietor of his person and capacities, and that any loss of such ownership is a loss of freedom. Thus the Levellers' claim for natural religious, civil and economic rights was based upon men's 'property in themselves'; upon the right to develop their capacities to the full unhindered by the state or other individuals. According to this theory, only those who enjoyed economic independence were truly free and this helps to explain the Levellers' refusal to give the vote to wage-earners and paupers; such men had lost the property in their own labour and forfeited their birthright. This concept of possessive individualism, in Macpherson's view, had unforeseen consequences. He writes: 'By putting an ill-defined but strongly asserted natural property right at the centre of their advocacy of the people's cause, they made it easy for Locke to confuse, in the general estimation, the equal right to property with the right to unlimited property, and thus to harness democratic sentiments to the Whig cause.' If this is true (one must always be cautious when dealing with the pedigrees of ideas) the Levellers had inadvertently contributed to the preservation of the privileges of those who had defeated them.

The Levellers failed. The sea-green ribbons appeared again briefly among the peasants and weavers of Somerset when they joined Monmouth's ill-starred rebellion, but the movement had long been dead. The landed classes, the exposure of whose interests and motives must stand, in the eyes of the historian, as one of the prime Leveller achievements, reasserted their dominance and set out confidently on another two hundred years of unchallenged political precedence. Perhaps the last word may be left with Richard Rumbold, onetime agitator and Rye House plotter, captured after taking part in Argyll's invasion of Scotland in 1685. On the scaffold, facing a traitor's death, he echoed the sentiments he and his comrades had made familiar in the maelstrom years of the English Revolution:

'I am sure there was no man born marked of God above another; for none comes into the world with a saddle on his back, neither any booted and spurred to ride him' (**13**).

Part Four

DOCUMENTS

RELIGIOUS TOLERATION

The Levellers first came together while opposing Presbyterian plans for an intolerant national church. This extract from An Appeale *(17 July 1647) by Richard Overton outlines the Leveller case for toleration.*

And as for matters of conscience or opinion about Religion or Worship, with which humane society, cohabitation, and safety may freely subsist and stand together, that doth not fall under the power of the Magisteriall sword, either for introduction and setlement, or for extirpation and subversion; for the limits of Magistracy extend no further than humanity, or humane subsistance, not to spirituallity, or spirituall being; and no further, than its owne nature extends, no further may its compulsive power be stretched: And this is the true distinction for matter of subjection, betwixt God and Caesar, and what is Gods wee must in the first place give unto God, and what is Caesars, in the second place, freely and readily we must give unto Caesar; the inward man is Gods prerogative, the outward man is mans prerogative; God is the immediate Lord over the inward, and mediately over the outward, but man is onely Lord over the outward, and though immediate thereover, yet but by Deputation or Commission from him who is thus both over the one and the other: And God who only knoweth the heart, and searcheth the reines, hath reserved the governation thereof to himself as his own prerogative, and the onely means which he useth in this kinde of Government, that by his Ministers must be dispensed, is onely by the word, not by the sword; for the sword pierceth but the flesh, it toucheth but the outward man, it cannot touch the inward; therefore where by the word (to wit by Doctrine or Argumentation) the proper means to work upon the intellectualls and affections a conversion, is not nor cannot be obtained, there no human compulsive power or force is to be used, either for plantation or extirpation.

From *Leveller Manifestoes of the Puritan Revolution* (**3**).

document 2

THE AGITATORS

In April and May 1647, the ordinary soldiers of the New Model elected representatives—'agitators'—in their struggle to obtain satisfaction of their grievances before demobilisation. When Parliment ordered disbandment on 25 May 1647 (the vote referred to in this letter) the agitators took the initiative and forced their officers to lead a general mutiny.

This letter, probably from one Lieutenant Chillenden of Whalley's regiment of horse, gives the agitators the latest news from London. Some of the ciphers are easy: 51 is London, 55 the army, 44 the agitators, and 43 a rendezvous.

Gentlemen,

My best respects. I rid hard and came to London by 4 this afternoone. The House hath ordered and voted the Army to be disbanded, Regiment by Regiment. The General's Regiment of Foote on Tuesday next to lay downe their Armes in Chelmsford Church, and they doe intend to send you down once more Commissioners to doe it of Lord and Commons; they will not pay more than two months pay, and after we be disbanded to state our Accompts and to be paid by the Excise in course. This is their good Vote, and their good vissible securitie. Pray, Gentlemen, ride night and day; wee will act here night and day for you. You must by all meanes frame a Petition in the name of all the Souldiers, to be presented to the Generall by you the Agitators, to have him in honour, justice and honestie, to stand by you, and to tell Skippon to depart the Army and all other Officers that are not right. . . .

Now, my Ladds, if wee worke like men wee shall doe well, and that in the hands of (52); and lett all the (44) be very instant that the (55) may be called to a (43) and that with speed; delay it not, by all meanes and be sure to stirre upp the Counties to Petition, and for their rights to make appeale to (55) to assist them. You shall heare all I can by the next. Soe till then I rest.

Yours till death,

From 51, 11 at night.   102.

From *The Clarke Papers* (1).

110

SOVEREIGNTY OF THE PEOPLE

At an early stage the Levellers claimed that sovereignty lies in the people. This is an extract from The Case of the Army truly stated *(15 October 1647), a comprehensive document which criticised the army leadership and sought to unite military and civilian malcontents behind the Levellers' radical constitutional proposals.* The Case of the Army *formed the basis for the* Agreement of the People *debated at Putney.*

Whereas all power is originally and essentially in the whole body of the people of this Nation, and whereas their free choice or consent by their Representors is the only originall of foundation of all just government; and the reason and end of the choice of all just Governors whatsoever is their apprehension of safety and good by them, that it be insisted upon possitively. That the supreame power of the peoples representors or Commons assembled in Parliament, be forthwith clearly declared as their power to make lawes, or repeale lawes, (which are not, or ought not to be unalterable) as also their power to call to an account all officers in this Nation whatsoever, for their neglect or treacheries in their trust for the peoples good, and to continue or displace and remove them from their offices, dignities or trust, according to their demerrits by their faithfulnesse or treacherie in the businesse or matters where with they are intrusted. And further, that this power to constitute any kind of governors or officers, that they shall judge to be for the peoples good, be declared, and that upon the aforesaid considerations it be insisted upon, that all obstructions to the freedome and equallitie of the peoples choice of their Representors, either by Pattents, Charters or usurpations, by pretended customes, be removed by these present Commons in Parliament, and that such a freedome of choice be provided for, as the people may be equally represented. This power of Commons in Parliament, is the thing against which the King hath contended, and the people have defended with their lives, and therefore ought now to be demanded as the price of their blood.

From *Leveller Manifestoes of the Puritan Revolution* (**3**).

document 4

THE LEVELLER CONSTITUTION

The Levellers rejected both monarchy and House of Lords and proposed that legislative and executive authority should be vested in a single chamber to be elected by a far wider franchise than that already in existence. This is an extract from the third Agreement of the People (*1 May 1649*), *published shortly before the final Leveller débâcle at Burford.*

. . . We the free People of England . . . do . . . agree to ascertain our Government, to abolish all arbitrary Power, and to set bounds and limits both to our Supreme, and all Subordinate Authority, and remove all known Grievances.

    And accordingly do declare and publish to all the world, that we are agreed as followeth,

1. That the Supreme Authority of England and the Territories therewith incorporate, shall be and reside henceforward in a Representative of the people consisting of four hundred persons, but no more; in the choice of whom (according to naturall right) all men of the age of one and twenty yeers and upwards (not being servants, or receiving alms, or having served the late King in Arms or voluntary Contributions) shall have their voices; and be capable of being elected to that Supreme Trust those who served the King being disabled for ten years only.

From *Leveller Manifestoes of the Puritan Revolution* (**3**).

INDIVIDUAL RIGHTS

The Levellers' individualism is shown by this extract from the first
Agreement of the People (*3 November 1647*). *Having proposed that
the Government should represent a far larger proportion of the population,
the Levellers reserved certain fundamental rights which the new Representative would not be able to infringe. Their own experiences in the
years 1646–1949 confirmed the Levellers' suspicion of central executive
authority and their emphasis on individual rights developed into a full-
scale programme of decentralisation.*

We declare . . . that the power of this, and all future Representatives of this Nation, is inferiour only to theirs who chuse
them, and doth extend, without the consent or concurrence
of any other person or persons; to the enacting, altering, and
repealing of Lawes; . . . And generally, to whatsoever is not
expresly, or implyedly reserved by the represented to themselves.
      Which are as followeth,
   1. That matters of Religion, and the wayes of Gods Worship,
are not at all intrusted by us to any humane power, because
therein wee cannot remit or exceed a tittle of what our Consciences dictate to be the mind of God, without wilfull sinne:
neverthelesse the publike way of instructing the Nation (so it be
not compulsive) is referred to their discretion.
   2. That the matter of impresting and constraining any of us to
serve in the warres, is against our freedome; and therefore we
do not allow it in our Representatives; the rather, because
money (the sinews of war) being alwayes at their disposall, they
can never want numbers of men, apt enough to engage in any
just cause.
   3. That after the dissolution of this present Parliament, no
person be at any time questioned for anything said or done, in
reference to the late publike differences, otherwise then in
execution of the Judgments of the present Representatives, or
House of Commons.
   4. That in all Laws made, or to be made, every person may be
bound alike, and that no Tenure, Estate, Charter, Degree,

113

Birth, or place, do confer any exemption from the ordinary Course of Legall proceedings, whereunto others are subjected. 5. That as the Laws ought to be equall, so they must be good, and not evidently destructive to the safety and well-being of the people.
These things we declare to be our native Rights . . .

THE PUTNEY DEBATES

The first Agreement of the People *was debated in the General Council of the Army at Putney in the late autumn of* 1647. *The crucial difference of opinion between the Levellers and the Grandees was over the question of the suffrage. Cromwell and Ireton claimed that an extension of the suffrage would threaten the very basis of the constitution, property itself. The Levellers, here represented by Rainsborough and Sexby, pointed out that the maintenance of the status quo would leave political power in the hands of the rich while those less fortunate, including the rank and file of the army, remained as unfree as before.*

Rainborow For my parte I thinke wee cannott engage one way or other in the Army if wee doe nott thinke of the people's liberties. If wee can agree where the liberty and freedome of the people lies, that will doe all.

Ireton I cannot consent soe farre . . .
. . . The law of God doth nott give mee propertie, nor the law of nature, but propertie is of humane Constitution. I have a propertie and this I shall enjoy. Constitution founds propertie. If either the thinge itt selfe that you presse (do destroy property), though I shall acquiesce in having noe propertie, yett I cannott give my heart or hand to itt; because itt is a thinge evill in ittself and scandalous to the world, and I desire this Army may bee free from both.

Sexby . . . Wee have engaged in this Kingdome and ventur'd our lives, and itt was all for this: to recover our birthrights and privileges as Englishmen, and by the arguments urged there is none. There are many thousands of us souldiers that have ventur'd our lives; wee have had little propriety in the Kingdome as to our estates, yett wee have had a birthright. Butt it seemes now except a man hath a fix't estate in this Kingedome, hee hath noe right in this Kingedome. I wonder wee were soe much deceived. If wee had nott a right to the Kingedome, wee were meere mercinarie souldiers . . .

From *The Clarke Papers* (**1**).

document 7

SOCIAL AND ECONOMIC DEMANDS

Early in their career the Levellers linked their constitutional ideas with far-reaching social and economic demands. This paragraph from the Petition of March 1647 shows the breadth of their programme. Law reform and the abolition of tithes had a wide appeal and were taken up by all radical groups during these years.

And although all new illegall Patents are . . . abolished, yet the oppressive Monopoly of Merchant-adventurers, and others, do still remain to the great abridgement of the liberties of the people, and to the extreme prejudice of all such industrious people as depend on cloathing, or other woollen manufacture, (it being the Staple commodity of this Nation) and to the great discouragement and disadvantage of all sorts of Tradesmen, Sea-faring-men, and hindrance of Shipping and Navigation. Also the old tedious and chargable way of deciding controversies, or suits in Law, is continued to this day, to the extreame vexation and utter undoing of multitudes of Families; a grievance as great and as palpable as any in the world. Likewise, that old, but most unequall punishment of male-factors, is still continued, whereby mens lives and liberties are as liable to the law, and corporall pains as much inflicted for small as for great offences, and that most unjustly upon the testimony of one witnesse, contrary both to the law of God, and common equity, a grievance very great, but litle regarded. Also tythes, and other enforced maintenance are still continued, though there be no ground for either under the Gospel; and though the same have occasioned multitudes of suites, quarrels and debates, both in former and latter times. In like maner, multitudes of poore distressed prisoners for debt, ly still un-regarded, in a most miserable and wofull condition throughout the Land, to the great reproach of this Nation. Likewise Prison-Keepers, or Goalers, are as presumptious as ever they were, both in receiving and detaining of Prisoners illegally committed, as cruell and inhumane to all, especially to such as are well-affected, as oppressive and extorting in their Fees, and are attended with under-officers, of such vile and un-

hristian demeanour, as is most abominable. Also thousands of
men and women are still (as formerly) permitted to live in
beggery and wickedness all their life long, and to breed their
children to the same idle and vitious course of life, and no
effectual meanes used to reclaim either, or to reduce them to
any vertue or industry.

From *Leveller Manifestoes of the Puritan Revolution* (**3**).

document 8

TRADESMEN SUPPORTERS

The tradesmen of London provided the backbone of the Levellers'
civilian support. Already impoverished by changes in the structure of
industry, the small craftsman found his hardships exacerbated by
heavy taxation and the economic distress of the years 1646–1649.
This extract from The mournfull Cryes of many thousand poor
Tradesmen, who are ready to famish through decay of Trade
(22 January 1648) gives an indication of the class appeal of some
Leveller propaganda.

Oh that the cravings of our Stomacks could be heard by the
Parliament and City! Oh that the Tears of our poor famishing
Babes were botled! Oh that their tender Mothers Cryes for
bread to feed them were ingraven in Brasse! . . .

O you Members of Parliament, and rich men in the City, that
are at ease, and drink Wine in Bowls, and stretch your selves
upon Beds of Down, you that grind our faces, and flay off our
skins, Will no man amonst you regard, will no man behold our
faces black with Sorrow and Famine? . . .

Oh ye great men of England, will not (think you) the
righteous God behold our Affliction, doth not he take notice
that you devour us as if our Flesh were Bread? . . . What then
are your rustling Silks and Velvets, and your glittering Gold
and Silver Laces? are they not the sweat of our brows, and the
wants of our backs and bellies?

Its your Taxes, Customs, and Excize, that compells the
Countrey to raise the price of food, and to buy nothing from us
but meer absolute necessaries; and then you of the City that
buy our Work, must have your Tables furnished, and your Cups
overflow; and therefore will give us little or nothing for our
Work, even what you please, because you know we must sell
for moneys to set our Families on work, or else we famish:
Thus our Flesh is that whereupon you Rich men live, and
wherewith you deck and adorn your selves. Ye great men, Is it
not your plenty and abundance which begets you Pride and
Riot? And doth not your Pride beget Ambition, and your
Ambition Faction, and your Faction these Civil broyles? What

else but your Ambition and Faction continue our Distractions
and Oppressions? Is not all the Controversie whose Slaves the
poor shall be?

From *Leveller Manifestoes of the Puritan Revolution* (**3**).

LEVELLER VIEW OF THE GRANDEES

By the spring of 1649 the Levellers were well on the road to defeat. The second Agreement *had been amended by the officers and shelved by the Rump; the king had been executed without any guarantees of a popularly-based constitution. In* The Hunting of the Foxes *(21 March 1649) Richard Overton turned savagely on the Grandees— 'Foxes in the habits of Saints'—and accused them of using the honest soldiers to further their own evil ambitions.*

O Cromwell! whither art thou aspiring? The word is already given out amongst their officers, That this Nation must have one prime Magistrate or Ruler over them; and that the General hath power to make a law to bind all the Commons of England: This was most daringly and desperately avowed at White-hall; and to this temper these Court-Officers are now a moulding, he that runs may read and fore-see the intent, a New Regality! And thus by their Machiavilian pretenses, and wicked practises, they are become masters and usurpers of the name of the Army, and of the name of the Parliament; under which Visors they have levell'd and destroyed all the Authority of this Nation: For the Parliament indeed and in truth is no Parliament, but a Representative Class of the Councel of War; and the Councel of War, but the Representative of Cromwel, Ireton, and Harrison; and these are the all in all of this Nation, which under these guises and names of Parliament, Army, General Councel, High Court, and Councel of State, play all the strange pranks that are play'd.

From *Leveller Manifestoes of the Puritan Revolution* (**3**).

Bibliography

DOCUMENTS

1 Firth, Sir C. H., ed. *The Clarke Papers*, The Camden Society, 1891–1901. The Clarke Manuscripts, which report the debates in the General Council of the Army, are essential to any study of the Levellers.

2 Woodhouse, A. S. P., ed. *Puritanism and Liberty*, Dent 1951. A newer edition of the Clarke Manuscripts, with modern spelling and punctuation, more readily available than Firth's pioneer work.

3 Wolfe, Don M., ed. *Leveller Manifestoes of the Puritan Revolution*, Nelson 1944. Includes the three versions of the *Agreement of the People*.

4 Haller, W., ed. *Tracts on Liberty in the Puritan Revolution, 1638–1647*, Columbia University Press 1934.

5 Haller, W. and Davies, G., ed. *The Leveller Tracts, 1647–1653*, Columbia University Press 1944.

GENERAL

6 Aston, T., ed. *Crisis in Europe, 1560–1660*, Routledge & Kegan Paul 1965. A collection of articles from *Past and Present* relevant to the thesis that there was a general crisis in the seventeenth century.

7 Gardiner, S. R. *History of the Great Civil War, 1642–1649*, Longmans 1893.

8 Gardiner, S. R. *History of the Commonwealth and Protectorate, 1649–1656*, Longmans 1903. Nos. (**7**) and (**8**) are still the best narrative histories of the period.

9 Hill, C. *The English Revolution 1640*, Lawrence & Wishart 1940. A Marxist interpretation of the Civil War, in which the Levellers appear as the petty bourgeoisie whose failure marks the failure of the revolution as a whole.

E

Bibliography

10 Hill, C. *The Century of Revolution, 1603–1714*, Nelson 1961.

11 Pearl, V. *London and the Outbreak of the Puritan Revolution* Oxford University Press 1961.

12 Roots, I. *The Great Rebellion, 1642–1660*, Batsford 1966.

STUDIES OF THE LEVELLERS

13 Brailsford, H. N. *The Levellers and the English Revolution*, ed. C. Hill, Cresset Press, 1961. A massive work, full of information, perhaps a little too sympathetic to its subject.

14 Frank, J. *The Levellers*, Harvard University Press 1955. Lays particular emphasis on the writings of Lilburne, Overton and Walwyn. Excellent bibliography.

15 Holorenshaw, H. *The Levellers and the English Revolution*, Gollancz 1939.

16 Pease, T. C. *The Leveller Movement*, American Historical Association, 1916.

RELIGION AND IDEAS

Books

17 Gooch, G. P. *English Democratic Ideas in the Seventeenth Century*, Harper Torchbook 1959.

18 Haller, W. *The Rise of Puritanism*, Columbia University Press 1938.

19 Haller, W. *Liberty and Reformation in the Puritan Revolution*, Columbia University Press 1963.
These two books by Haller are indispensable for an understanding of the Levellers' religious background.

20 Hill, C. *Intellectual Origins of the English Revolution*, Oxford University Press 1965.

21 Hill, C. *Puritanism and Revolution*, Secker & Warburg 1958. Several relevant essays here, notably 'The Norman Yoke'.

22 Jordon, W. K. *The Development of Religious Toleration in England*, Harvard University Press 1932–40.

23 Macpherson, C. B. *The Political Theory of Possessive Individualism*, Oxford University Press 1962. Disposes of the notion that the Levellers advocated manhood suffrage. See also No. (**31**).

24 Petegorsky, D. W. *Left-Wing Democracy in the English Civil War: A Study in the Social Philosophy of Gerrard Winstanley*, Gollancz 1940.

25 Robertson, D. B. *The Religious Foundations of Leveller Democracy*, Kings Crown Press, Columbia University 1951.

26 Schenk, W. *The Concern for Social Justice in the Puritan Revolution*, Longmans 1948.

27 Tawney, R. H. *Religion and the Rise of Capitalism*, Murray 1926.

28 Walzer, M. *The Revolution of the Saints*, Weidenfeld & Nicolson 1966.

Articles

29 Cole, A. 'The Quakers and the English Revolution', *Past and Present* 10, 1956; also in (**6**).

30 Hexter, J. H. 'The problem of the Presbyterian Independents', *American Historical Review*, xlviii, 1938; also in *Reappraisals in History*, Longmans 1961.

31 Laslett, P. Review of Macpherson's *The Political Theory of Possessive Individualism*, *The Historical Journal*, vii, no. 1. Criticism of Macpherson's view of the Leveller suffrage proposals.

32 Thomas, K. V. 'Women and the Civil War sects', *Past and Present* 13, 1958; also in (**6**).

SOCIAL AND ECONOMIC

Books

33 Campbell, M. *The English Yeoman in the Tudor and Stuart Age*, Yale University Press 1942.

34 Hill, C. *Society and Puritanism in Pre-Revolutionary England*, Secker & Warburg 1964.

35 Laslett, P. *The World We Have Lost*, Methuen 1965. A sociological approach to the period.

36 Lipson, E. *The Economic History of England*, vol. 2, 6th edn., A. and C. Black 1956.

37 Stone, L. *Social Change and Revolution in England, 1540–1640*, Longmans 1965. A guide to the present state of the parties in the controversy over the social and economic origins of the Civil War. Useful bibliography.

38 Unwin, G. *Industrial Organisation in the Sixteenth and Seventeenth Centuries*, Oxford, Clarendon Press 1904.

Bibliography

39 Wedgwood, C. V. *The Common Man in the Great Civil War*, Leicester University Press 1957.

Articles

40 James, M. 'The political importance of the tithes controversy in the English Revolution, 1640–1660' *History* xxvi, 1941.

41 Stone, L. 'The educational revolution in England, 1560–1640', *Past and Present* 28, 1964.

42 Stone, L. 'Social mobility in England, 1500–1700', *Past and Present* 33, 1966.

MILITARY

43 Firth, Sir C. H. *Cromwell's Army*, 3rd edn. Methuen 1921.

44 Solt, L. F. *Saints in Arms: Puritanism and Democracy in Cromwell's Army*, Oxford University Press 1959.

BIOGRAPHY

45 Ashley, M. *John Wildman: Plotter and Postmaster*, Cape 1947.

46 Firth, Sir C. H. *Oliver Cromwell and the Rule of the Puritans in England*, New York: The Knickerbocker Press 1900 (available in World's Classics, O.U.P.).

47 Gibb, M. A. *John Lilburne, A Christian Democrat*, Lindsay Drummond, 1947.

48 Gregg, P. *Free-born John: A Biography of John Lilburne*, Harrap 1961.

49 Hill, C. *Oliver Cromwell, 1658–1958*, Historical Association Pamphlet, G.38.

50 Williamson, H. R. *Four Stuart Portraits*, Evans 1949. Includes a short study of Rainsborough.

There are no full-length biographies of Walwyn or Overton. Firth treated them both in the *Dictionary of National Biography*.

Index

Index

Index